MW00748425

Healing a Broken Man

Along the Broken Road

Healing the Soul, Skyclad – Volume 3

Other books by Robert G. Longpré

Through a Jungian Lens series (Psychology):
Volume 1 – Swamplands: The Dark Night of the Soul, 2009
Volume 2 – Tunnel Vision: Journey on the Prairies, 2009
Volume 3 – Discovering the Hero Within, 2009
Volume 4 – Sol and Luna: On Becoming Whole, 2010
Volume 5 – Individuation and Consciousness, 2011

Healing the Soul series (Autobiographical):
Volume 1 - A Broken Boy on the Broken Road, 2014
Volume 2 - On the Broken Road to a Magical Other, 2013
Volume 3 – Healing a Broken Man, 2016

Skyclad Poetry series:
Volume 1 - By the Sea and on the Prairies, 2013
Volume 2 - At Home and in Nature. 2014
Volume 3 - She, He, We, 2015

Skyclad Novel series:
Volume 1 – A Small Company of Pilgrims, 2014

Other books (Social History):
Sagitawak: Bicentennial History of Ile a la Crosse, 1977
Crazy Emigrant: The story of Nicholas Berdowitz, 1979

Healing a Broken Man

Along the Broken Road

Healing the Soul Skyclad – Volume 3

Robert G. Longpré

Retired Eagle Books

April, 2016

Dedication

Though we may think that we do the work of healing the "self" on our own, the truth is that there are always "others" who make the journey with us. Maureen and my children, Noelle, Natasha, and Dustin, have all had a vital part in the process of helping me put the broken pieces of my psyche being back together. This book is dedicated to them. This book is also dedicated to my six grandchildren in hopes that they learn that it is okay to be broken, for the pieces can be welded back together making them stronger men. This book is also for all the others who need to put the pieces back together again.

Robert G. Longpré

"whatever reality may be, it will to some extent be shaped by the lens through which we see it". – James Hollis, Jungian Analyst, The Middle Passage, 1993.

Retired Eagle Books
Box 423 Elrose,
Saskatchewan, Canada S0L 0Z0

ISBN-13: 978-1530749270

Cover Photo

The cover photo needs some explanation in order for it to make sense. There are five images in the photo collage. The top left image is one that I have called *The Magical Other*. The book begins with life lived with my Magical Other, the woman who was the place holder for my soul. The top right image shows the practice of meditation, one of the vital strategies that I have used in my journey of healing. The bottom right image illustrates the intellectual part of my journey of healing, the work of Carl Gustav Jung that finds a place for soul and spirituality in the practice of depth psychology. The bottom left image presents a scene from my journey through nature while skyclad in which nature, the sun, and the elements serve as part of the healing process, a physical dimension to match the intellectual and spiritual dimension. The central image is yin yang, the union of the masculine and feminine aspects of a whole person.

The second aspect of the cover photo that needs some explanation is the use of different hues for four of the photos. The reason for these hues – black focus, white focus, yellow focus, and red focus – has to do with the four stages of psychological transformation as a healing process. The dark stage is called negredo and it is characterised with a loss of life force – depression. The second stage is called albedo, the whitening stage. In this stage, there is a gaining back of energy as one moves from darkness into awareness, typically through working with a guide such as a therapist or analyst. The third stage is called citrinitas, the yellowing stage. It marks the removal of projections, especially those projections that place one's positive qualities onto others. It's like taking off the rose-coloured glasses that blind one to the realities of others while keeping one blind with regards to oneself. In other words, one gains real wisdom that awareness of self and other in the world. The last stage, rubedo, is the reddening stage. This is where the self is "reborn" as a whole person. In simple terms, one has finally got his or her "shit together." It is only when this process has repeated over and over again that one can finally be able to see both self and others with clear eyes. It is only at this point that a union of opposites, the shadow and the light within which allows us to become whole, perhaps even holy.

Introduction

The sky is wild this morning. One minute it is dark with ominous clouds flying by as if they are on a freeway, and the next minute there is glorious sunshine. The speed at which this is all happening makes the mind swirl. The wind has been blowing all night following a long period of rain yesterday, late afternoon and all evening; and it is still blowing strong, creating whitecaps and pounding waves along the shoreline. Sometimes nature serves as a good metaphor for what is happening within one's psyche. I know that in today's case, nature mirrors the stormy seas within me.

I didn't sleep well and it wasn't because of the rain or the wind. Rather, it was because of the stirring of shadowy contents within me, stuff that lies below the surface of my awareness in a place called the unconscious. In this unconscious world within, which I usually access at night in dreams, I usually find myself as both the hero and the villain of the inner dramas. And usually, I am there, naked in those dreams.

I was asked more than once why I was a naturist, why I needed to be naked when the rest of the world, the *civilized* world, was doing quite well with their clothes on. I wasn't able to give a satisfactory answer nor did I think that there ever could be a satisfactory answer in terms of having another person who is not a naturist, understand and accept my reasoning. Of course, saying that, I open myself to the possibility of being very wrong. I don't really have an excuse for not finding the right words to answer this question, even if it is just for myself. This book is an attempt, in part, to answer that question.

Because of my long involvement with depth psychology, I knew that the answers did exist, somewhere deep within my psyche, my answers. So this morning, I opened up the door to the question during my time for meditation which then lasted longer than usual. It was essential for me to let the question stew for a while, allow the contents within to become stirred up in the darkness of the unconscious. Later in the morning, after sitting for a while in silence with my morning coffee, not actually thinking but also not banishing thinking, I went for a long, two hour walk along the beach. I refused to force an answer but I also left an opening, much like an opening in the clouds for the sun to peek through, an opening for whatever words needed to come to consciousness.

As a child I was sexually abused, emotionally abused, and physically abused by my parents. The sexual abuse extended to include my maternal grandfather and more than one parish priest. I was a docile child, the eldest of nine children that eventually filled our homes. As I understood it, while growing up it was my job to please others, to take care of others, to put others before myself. I forgave my parents for their part in the abuses before they both passed away, unspoken forgiveness for we never talked about what had happened. But long before their deaths, I had banished knowledge of the abuse into prisons buried deep within me and then forgot about them. It was an instinctual and unconscious act so that I could survive and be somewhat functional as an adult. Having forgotten the abuse of the past, I was able to include my parents in the lives of my children's as grandparents, grandparents at distance.

The behaviour patterns I learned in early childhood, continued until years after I was married with children of my own. I carried over the patterns influencing how I interacted within the family in which I was husband and father. It carried over into my career as an educator, coach and then as counsellor to students, staff and people from within my community. I was well trained to put others first and do my utmost best to be a good father, a good husband, brother-in-law, coach, and neighbour. This was a story I knew well, one that I wrestled with through midlife and my own psychoanalysis and therapy. But where did the almost primal urge to naturalism come from?

It was soon after being sexually abused by my maternal grandfather, the last time I was sexually abused as a youth that I found myself in a quiet meadow behind our house in the country, in a nearby small forest with a book of poetry. It was a warm, late spring day, about six months after this sexual abuse. Feeling the warmth of the sun, and listening to the words of classical poetry, I soon found myself naked. Over the next two years, my last two years at home, I took every opportunity, weather permitting to hide in this tiny forest meadow in order to be *free* and that freedom saw me skyclad, clothed only in the sun's rays.

After leaving home, I found other opportunities to be naked, especially the opportunity of sleeping in the nude in order to recapture that sense of freedom. A job at the other end of the country found me enjoying social nudity in swimming pools and saunas with my co-workers, other young adults. The exhilaration of body freedom acted as a sort of barrier and filter that banished my history of being abused into dungeons deep within my psyche.

Yet now in my senior years, the pull to nudity is again strong. So I look to these roots in hopes of making sense of that urge to be nude. It finally dawned on me that it is when I am nude where I finally claim control of my body, control of my identity, control of my sexuality. My body is not about pleasing others, making life easier for others. Do I allow the needs of others to dictate what I do or don't do with my body? It all comes down to control. Am I in control or do I defer control to others? If the past is the deciding factor, and it was for at least sixty years, the answer has always been that the needs of others always trumped my needs.

Now, in my sixties, I am saying this is my body and I will care for it, and my identity, and my psyche as best I can. I will not be a child and give control of myself to another. I am a man, not a child victim continuing to seek approval, seeking to please others while disregarding my *self*.

I wonder if this is an answer, or just the beginning of an answer?

Robert G. Longpré

Part One

Ignorance is Bliss

"We are all socialized to serve and maintain the collective, family structures and social institutions that have a life of their own but require the repeated sacrifice of the individual to sustain them."

James Hollis – <u>Under Saturn's Shadow</u>

Chapter One

In trying to put the pieces of my psyche back together, the pieces that were scattered through several decades of life, I have taken to using nudity as part of my personal healing process. As a trained counsellor, I have alternated between doing self-analysis and going to a trusted Jungian analyst for expert guided analysis. The process of Jungian analysis has much in common with a conscious approach to entering a naturist experience, as well as a dedicated practice of mindful meditation. With these three processes working together, there is an uncovering to bring light what otherwise would always hidden in darkness, hidden in the shadows. It is not enough simply to uncover what is hidden in the shadows beneath our memories, there is a need to focus on what is discovered without judgment, accept it as having happened and having shaped our responses to life as an adult, and then moving on with life. One needs to see what is hidden there beneath fear, and then to realise that what is uncovered is a more honest, a fuller version of the self, of who and what one is.

Last night, while I was sleeping, or perhaps in that middle place between sleep and wakefulness, I thought about the validity of using nudity, that is naturism, as part of my healing process. I could make a good case for using meditation for my therapy, and an even better case for getting help from a mental health professional.

How could I justify using nudity when the world I knew was so against nudity, so afraid of it? That question rattled me. Knowing my history, knowing that I had turned to being nude when I felt like my life was falling apart, the more important question now becomes, 'How could I not justify what had worked, what continues to work and have me become a saner, more balanced person?'

And now, I am writing this book that details my use of Jungian psychology and analysis, Buddhist meditation, and naturism working together to assist in my healing – the healing of the mind, body, spirit, soul - a holistic healing. I find myself entering into a more conscious awareness of what being nude is doing me as an individual.

Chapter Two

I began the second book in this series with a scene from behind a farm house on an acreage outside of Ottawa, a scene in which I was struggling with a crisis that had to do with yet one more sexual abuse by an adult that I had trusted, my maternal grandfather. In that scene, I was naked. There was nothing conscious about that act, no deliberate choice to get out of my clothes simply to be nude. It was as if the body, my body had its own knowledge, knew what it needed to do rather than have me destroy myself out of shame. I was suicidal and struggling to make it through each day, and struggling even more for survival with the arrival of night. I was being unconsciously drawn into experiencing healing through nudity.

The particular location for that first nude healing experience was a safe and private opening in the treed quarter of land behind the acreage home we had lived in at the time. Before long it that initial experience was followed up with other nude experiences in other locations. These experiences took place in the 1960s, a time when there was less negative response to nudity by our culture in general.

It was also the era of flower children and hippies, the generation of love, flowers, and peace movements. During the summer of 1967, I found myself sunbathing by the river where others were laying naked in the sunshine. I stayed closer to the trees as though the trees would be my protectors not because I was ashamed of being nude, but because I didn't trust people, people had a tendency to hurt me. I stayed in a mentally private space even though I was intimately exposed to the eyes of the others who were also sunbathing. I didn't know it at the time, but those other sunbathers were there for themselves, not to stare critically at me.

That summer has long passed and new traumatic events had been experienced while old traumatic experiences were buried deeper into the most remote corners of my psyche and eventually forgotten. The abuses, the long history of abuses had turned me into a furtive and fearful person, a young man who was afraid of shadows and afraid of people. I had already begun to suffer Post Traumatic Stress Disorder.

I finally left my parent's home and made my way into the outer world. I left childhood and entered into a different world of music, youth, and freedom. And, I entered into a world where nudity among other people was experienced in a non-sexual context though there was a sexual under-current for some of the others I encountered.

In time, my past vanished from my memories. I was able to enter into adulthood without consciously carrying the baggage of my childhood and youth. The experiences of nudity were continuing to work at repairing my sense of self, my need for control of myself. I didn't have access to mental health services at that time, nor did I think I needed them with the past locked away. All that I had as an unconscious mental health strategy was my trusting to my intuition. Unconsciously, I listened to my inner self and I slowly began to heal.

Working with other young adults, male and female, who were my age, and who were also broken youth with their own unspoken wounds; I found myself engaging in shared moments of social nudity. We shared sauna experiences, swimming pool experiences, and incidental moments when one or more were nude. There arose a level of trust between us. These experiences were not complicated by any boyfriend and girlfriend relationships. We were travelling workmates who cherished our escape from the real world and our shattered pasts.

Then I met my wife in the late summer of 1970, on the September long week-end.

Chapter Three

I fell in love. It's as simple as that. It was like a story from a fairy tale with both of us experiencing *love at first sight*. A twelfth century Persian poet captured it well with these words:

> *Out beyond ideas of wrongdoing and rightdoing,*
> *there is a field. I'll meet you there.*
>
> *When the soul lies down in that grass,*
> *the world is too full to talk about.*
> *Ideas, language, even the phrase each other*
> *doesn't make any sense.*
> *- Rumi, "Open Secret"*

We were two strangers who had met late one rainy afternoon; and who, before the end of that same day, declared that we would marry each other and live together, forever. There was nothing in that declaration that made any sense at all when looked at from a rational perspective. Whatever we did and said, was done and said because we were in love. We were fully vulnerable as we both allowed the strangeness of each other to enter intimately into each other's world.

Forty-five years later, I am still married to this same woman. In the hours between meeting and our commitment to each other, we had not talked about our pasts. No secrets were divulged. Yet somehow, there was something about her in which I took refuge, and something about me that encouraged her to take refuge in me. Taking refuge in each other. I doubt that either of us had the slightest thought that we were taking refuge, or that we needed to take refuge, or even what taking refuge really meant. It was simple in our eyes back then, we had simply fallen in love.

But, what was this thing called love at first sight? It wasn't based on what we knew of the stranger we had just met. I knew nothing about her, nor did she know anything about me. We met as strangers with no shared history, yet only hours after meeting each other, we agreed to marry each other. What I did know of her is perhaps best explained as a feeling within me. What she knew of me was a feeling within her.

These things we hold inside of us, these unconscious feelings are mirrored in the other person. It is as if we have clothed the other person with our ideas and our feelings. In depth psychology, the act of creating an image of another based on our ideas and feelings is called *casting projections.* James Hollis, a Jungian analyst, wrote that "all relationships, *all relationships,* begin in projection." In other words, I fell in love with an image which I had projected on this young woman, and she had done the same with me.

I know, it doesn't sound so romantic when said this way. Regardless of the psychological background behind romantic love, what we both knew and understood was simply that we were truly in love with each other; and, we took that understanding as a fact. Based on that fact, we began a relationship that has lasted forty-five years to date. Needless to say, for us, as for all couples, the magical glow of romantic love would hit a bumpy and twisted and broken road in the years that followed falling in love at first sight.

So, what was it about me that had me fall in love with a person like her? And what was it about her that existed for me to cast projections and have them stick? If those projections had nothing to catch onto, there would have been no relationship. Projections unconsciously cast out need hooks in order to be caught. I can only answer based on my own history and psychological makeup. Only by understanding what was operating within me, would I be able to understand how and why I came unravelled at the seams, why I suffered a midlife crisis that threatened our marriage, my sanity, and even my life; depended upon the answer to, 'Why this woman?'.

To understand the present, I would have to go back to the beginning where I had unconsciously created a personal understanding of my world based on my child's perception of the people and events from that distant past. As children, things happen to all of us, all the time; and things happen all around us. Unfortunately, for some children, too many children, there is trauma involved. James Hollis explained this in a way that set a foundation for what is to occur in later life:

> *"If we have found myself essentially powerless against the Other, and what child has not, then how I am to comport*

myself in order to manage this distress? If I have routinely been invaded by abuse, verbal, emotional, sexual, or have more commonly been at the mercy of the moods and emotional vagaries of the parent, so I am inclined to identify with the Other."[1]

Hollis uses the word 'Other' to represent a person who has power, a person who has control because a child is powerless, or when we give up power and control to the other when we fall in love with someone, a Magical Other. Sometimes this 'Other' is not motivated by love. The control by those who abuse us, gives us a sense that these abusers have a magical power that would destroy us if we don't obey. We give these others authority rather than resist, and in our minds we must so that we can survive and perhaps even thrive. They become either evil villains or superheroes.

My story is filled with all of the forms of abuse that Hollis mentioned in his book. My identification with both mother and father, had shaped my responses to other men and women. They were my models of who to be and who not to be as an adult male. They were also my models of relationship. I learned what to hold close and what to fear in relationships to other men and women. And without knowing it, the seeds had been planted in my unconscious psyche which would direct and define the search for connection with what could best be called my 'Magical Other.' Meeting my wife, I met that magical other, a person that filled my unconscious needs for relationship which had been established in the earliest years of my life.

We all have these templates which we use to define and understand our world and the worlds of others. These templates are embedded deep within us. Unknown to us, each person we meet on the path of life is measured against these templates which are then used to identify friends and enemies. We follow the scripted patterns coded into these templates, as we connect with others of our own gender and with others of the opposite gender. This is how relationships with lovers, with children, with friends and enemies, with colleagues

---

[1] Hollis, James, <u>The Eden Project</u>, 1998, p. 23.

and supervisors, and everyone else who enters into our lives are forged.

Of course, I am no different than anyone else when it comes to having the scripts and templates that were created in the distant past, serve as the foundation for how I would live my life and how I would relate to people as an adult. My childhood experiences of powerlessness, had set a path for my journey through the rest of my life.

There were two basic paths that I could have followed based on my experiences as a child and youth. On one hand, I could have carved out a life of being a powerful figure with power over others like my father, and to some extent like my mother. On the other hand, I could have shifted to pleasing others rather than dominating them. By the time I was four years old, the path of pleasing others had been chosen for it seemed to be the best path to follow in order to survive.

I had unconsciously followed the latter path, a path that I have lived from an early age, a path that became an automatic way of being in relationship with others and the world. Again, Hollis explains this:

> "Since the child felt powerless in the face of the Other who was yet the source of well-being, so it learns to be pleasing, mollifying or overly responsible for the well-being of others." [2]

And it was this embedded way of being that marked my life. I *knew* that if I didn't *please* that I would suffer at the hands of my father. That subordination to male authority with the need to please marked me for sexual abuse by a priest by the time I was seven. With my mother's needs not being taken care of, her emotional and sexual needs, I again saw that only through pleasing her could I survive her anger and vengeance. And so it went on as the years passed with more sexual abuse by other priests, manipulation by my mother so that I took over the care of my younger siblings to avoid pain. I pleased all who might have power over me by being the *good child.*

---

[2] p. 24

So, it shouldn't come as a surprise that how I dealt unconsciously with the real powerlessness of my childhood, would strongly influence how I had dealt with other people in my adulthood. Without knowing it, I chose, or should I say, gravitated towards relationships with others who had been wounded, others who had been powerless with their own histories and scripts to follow. I had a role of nurturing that was valued. And when I dared to change my way of relating to those others, I would end up in trouble, literally and figuratively.

Imagine two people falling in love, drawn together as if life depended upon it, as though there was a guiding force somewhere in the universe making sure that they met. Love at first sight felt exactly like that. There was no doubt, no wondering or hesitation. Unaware of the dynamics that are working beneath the level of our awareness, we settled into the coming together. With time passing, it seemed the closer we got, there was another force that began pushing us apart. Of course, as mature adults we all understand the ups and downs of relationship. And, in spite of our best efforts, we got caught on the rollercoaster of attraction and repulsion. Hollis describes this dynamic as:

> *"a ballet of approach and avoidance, where one partner needs reassuring closeness and the other is more comfortable with distance. One draws close seeking reassurance, while the other, feeling invaded, draws back, raising the anxiety level of both."[3]*

We met. We fell in love. We took refuge in each other. And, we began our own dance, our own ballet. Falling in love with each other, we fell into a place where we each found what we needed at that time, a safe place, perhaps even a sacred place. And like other star-struck lovers, we would have a price to pay for this in the future.

---

[3] p. 25-26

Chapter Four

Falling in love confirmed a value for myself that had begun with my naked protest behind my parent's home in the country, a protest against being sexually abused, against all of the abuse I lived with, against the power of authority. Being in love and being loved in return, I was protected and I offered protection. Under the spell of love, I learned to see my body and mind as beautiful. For the first time in my life, sex wasn't invasive nor did it leave me feeling ashamed. My sexual identity as a man had been resolved. I learned how to see and how to feel in a relationship, I learned how to trust myself and my Magical Other with my body and my mind.

We were in love and that love coloured our world. Without conscious intending to, as time passed, I began to test this love. Was this love unconditional? What were there boundaries that I had to learn in order for the love given to me to last? As a youth I had learned about unconditional love, but even the highest form of unconditional love, which was portrayed in Catholicism through Jesus, was conditional. Do it my way, or it's the highway. If I didn't do it right, I would be condemned forever to Hell. Jesus or God sounded more like my father than an all-loving deity. Was I right to trust my magical other unconditionally? Or, would there be hell to pay if I didn't get it right?

Our first spring together, assuming unconditional love and the trust that came with it, I dared to be skyclad during some of our nature walks through farmland pastures near her family's farm. My nudity didn't erupt into an issue – we were in love and love accepts everything that doesn't destroy. Unconditional love between us was given and received. There was no need for any explanations. We told each other through our words and deeds who we were, at least as much as we could without digging into our pasts.

I had found a safe shelter in my new relationship. I grew stronger and more confident in myself. I risked stepping out of my comfort zone of pleasing others in order to pursue denied dreams. I was testing the boundaries of my own templates. I went to university and became a teacher.

The dream deferred of becoming a teacher was drawn out of me by my wife. She could tell that there was more that I needed than was given to me by my work as a government clerk at that time. She encouraged me and gave me confidence to risk making my dream come true. So, two years after we met, I began to take university classes in southern British Columbia, at a university that accepted mature students.

During the year of university classes in Nelson, British Columbia I again engaged in naturist experiences when we were alone in the forested foothills of the local mountains. Again, the response was unconditional acceptance. We were in love. I took part in a social naturist experience during the winter at the home of one of my university professors. With snow on the mountain slopes where he lived with his wife, we tumbled and rolled in the snow after being cooked in the professor's sauna. We laughed at ourselves and the others who were with us. We were nothing more than grown up children having innocent fun.

In early 1973, when the snow had retreated and we were once again hiking down mountain paths and trails, we stumbled upon a hippy commune. We were invited in to the commune where we got to have tea and a meal. And, later in the afternoon, we were introduced to meditation. Another piece that I would need for my mental survival in the future was falling into place.

Having succeeded with my first year of classes in Nelson and with agreement from my wife, I decided to relocate to a university where I could pursue my dream of teaching indigenous, First Nations people. My family had deep roots in the indigenous people of Canada going back more than three hundred years. I had Abenaki, Mohawk and Ojibway roots going back centuries, mixed in with my French ancestry.

My father and his father had hidden the truth of our First Nations roots, denying those indigenous roots. In spite of those denials, the whispers behind the scenes as I grew up told me a different truth. I vowed I would make being indigenous something to be proud of. I affirmed being a Métis, with the intention of becoming a teacher majoring in indigenous education. Being in love and being loved in return had given me the courage to be authentic. My self-identity had expanded as I took that small piece out of my shadowy past and brought it into the light as something to be proud of.

We moved to Saskatoon, Saskatchewan in the summer of 1973. I registered in the College of Education with the plan of majoring in First Nation studies with the objective of teaching middle years students. I had earned a few scholarships at Nelson and proven that I was more than capable at university. I had come to believe in myself as a capable and intelligent young man.

I took on the challenges of the larger university and continued to excel at my studies. As was the case in Nelson, my peer group was made up of young professors and instructors, as well as a few other older students. Like Icarus flying high, I was soon soaring almost out of control with my head held high in the clouds of academic life. I left my body and I left my wife sitting almost abandoned while I competed for honours as though I was hunting trophies. I finally recognised what I was doing, recognised it when I saw the hurt within her.

The Philosopher and His Maureen

Taking for granted your need and your warmth
Taking for granted, tomorrow
I sit silently with a book in my hand
And I silently, so silently, leave you.

Gone to mountains of Philosophy and men
Gone in pursuit of the eternal
Nietzsche, Teilhard de Chardin, Spinoza, and Buddha
Beckon to the fringes of my mind.

Racing through the myths of other men's dreams
Racing through their pain and strife
My spirit soars in recognition of kinship
Then, seeing you, I fall back to earth.

You sit there painfully waiting for my return to you
Waiting for my return to the present hoping it won't be long
And you, so quiet, so sad, and so calm

You who I call my wife and best friend

You sit still waiting, looking for my eyes to see you
Hoping that I don't see you cry.

I drop my book and walk two million miles
Back to you and your essence grounded in reality
I walk back to hold you close and breath your essence
That tells me you are the only truth.

In spite of my soaring ego, Maureen and I held together. We were in love and that love was unconditional. We still had our plans that we had created together to guide us. We planned for the year to come when I would take a teaching position somewhere in the northern part of the province. We had dreams of becoming parents but we both needed the security of my having a steady job before making that dream come true.

Before the end of the second month of classes I had been given a contract to teach in the northern part of the province at a school located in Camsell Portage. The pressure was off for finding a job. We were both excited and motivated by this coming future. All I had to do at this point, was to focus on my classes and ensure that I got a teaching certificate.

Before winter, we both began to meditate. A young professor and his wife who had become friends with us, were going to try Transcendental Meditation which had been advertised at the university. I began to think that meditation might help to bring me back to earth and that it would help me be a better husband. I had discovered Buddhism years earlier, while a teenager in Ottawa. As I understood it then, Buddhism was more about psychology than about religion. I didn't know why I was intolerant and resistant to religions at that time, especially when I knew that I had been very religious as a child. What I read in the few Buddhist books I had come across, mixed in with what I had learned from philosophy, was pointing me toward a spiritual rather than a religious attitude to life. Meditation became a vital part of my days in spite of the fact that I didn't quite buy into Transcendental Meditation dogma.

I had taken up a more serious interest in photography during that year in Saskatoon, and I set up a darkroom in our basement. Between my relentless quests for recognition at the university, the practice of meditation, and learning about Buddhist ideas, along with an immersion into photography, naturism had disappeared. Since it had been an unconscious response, rather than a conscious choice, I didn't think of its absence. It returned into the shadow contents of my unconscious. I was too busy, too full of life for the shadows of the past that lurked at the edges of consciousness. The wounds of the past had fully disappeared from my awareness. It was time to live a full outer life fully in the present.

When I was assured of my teaching certificate after passing the final practicum on a First Nation's reserve, we celebrated by intentionally conceiving our first child. Life just couldn't get any better than it was at that time. I had a job, a profession. We were going to be parents. We were in love. We had it all.

At the end of August, 1974, we moved into the small village of Camsell Portage, the northernmost village in the province of Saskatchewan. I was employed as a teacher and as a principal of a two-room school in the community that was a mixture of Treaty and Métis people. I taught, hunted, worked on my photographs, wrote, and hiked with wife. With the hours filled to overflowing, meditation faded into the distance like naturism, one of those "I used to do" things that get abandoned along the journey of life.

Our first daughter was born soon after the New Year. My wife and I became even closer if that could have been possible, the ultimate bond that blended lovers into parents. Parenting was shared between both of us. I had more experience with babies and child care and shared what I knew. I abandoned most of my intellectual projects to be more present with my tiny family. I was filled to the brim with the roles of teacher, principal, friend, husband and father.

In the fall of 1975, there was a disturbance in our life as a young family. I was transferred out of Camsell Portage. We left the place we had envisioned would be our home for many years to come. Neither of us had any idea why we had to move. My first response was of wondering 'What I had done wrong? How had I screwed up?

The setback had stirred up ghosts from the past. Those ghosts blamed me for the situations I had found myself in when I got into trouble. I had no doubt that I had caused this to happen, I just didn't know how or why? We were both upset with the swiftness of the change that took us from our friends who had become our northern family. Yet, we both knew that there wasn't any choice, no way of undoing the decisions others had made.

We found ourselves transferred to a new community, a Métis town called Ile-a-la-Crosse, at the end of the Thanksgiving Day weekend. I was placed into the senior teacher position working with high school students as a teacher of History and English.

I learned later in the year that the reason for being placed in Ile-a-la-Crosse had been about politics. The politics of education behind the scenes had seen me lent to this school which was in a different school division. My Director of Education, the man who had hired me two years earlier, had lent me to his brother, who was principal of the school in Ile-a-la-Crosse, for the remainder of the school year. When the year was over, I was to be placed back into another school administered by my Director. Power and powerlessness. Both of us were reminded of our true vulnerability. Knowing we weren't going to be able to stay in this new community of Isle-a-la-Crosse, we were slow to make friends.

Not having to take on the role of principal in the large school, I found myself focused on the courses and the students I taught. I blossomed as a teacher while working with the young adults in the high school, something that I hadn't expected after having done all of my training with younger students. My students responded positively to my passion for teaching and willingly attempted the numerous creative assignments of poetry and drama. I gave them constant approval for their efforts, including putting their work on display for the community. My senior English class worked together with me to write and produce a play based on another famous play. They made changes to the original play in order to reflect their community, and their stories. Their successes and increased confidence were noticed in the community. I was seen as the reason for their success and as a result, I was asked to write the town's bicentennial history book. It was going to be my first paid piece of writing. In spite of all the poems, newspaper editorials, and essays, I had written and published in the past, I was finally beginning to see myself as a legitimate writer.

Though the town and the school had given me validation as a teacher and writer, we were both looking forward to living in a small village again, where I would again be a principal and teacher. Though we wouldn't be returning to the same northern village, we had hopes that we would be returning to another quiet, northern paradise. We wanted to have another child. With the decision made, we deliberately conceived our second child.

The third school in three years was a challenge that was unwelcome. We had both wanted to establish roots. The village of Sturgeon Landing had a violent past which simmered just below the surface. Its darkness was ever-present. In a way, that darkness felt familiar to me though I didn't think about why it felt familiar; for, it was just a faint echo of the forgotten past. Curiously, I thrived and met the challenges that the village presented. I felt confident in spite of the chaos. I felt anything but fear and powerlessness; and, I was treated as powerful and even respected force in the community.

For my wife it was different story. She didn't have the same sense of personal power that I felt. She felt real fear, especially on those occasions when I flew off to attend conferences and she was left alone with our little girl with another baby on the way. During one such conference absence, she was unpleasantly surprised by someone prowling around the house during the night, walking past our bedroom window. Her fears had her in a panic situation when I had confronted angry and drunken locals who had appeared in front of our house armed with rifles. They were calling out a police officer who had been having an evening meal with us. I had stepped outside to deal with this situation, unarmed. As there had already been a series of murders and deaths in the community, she believed that I was doing the wrong thing by confronting them. Yet I felt invulnerable and that was enough for me; and, that attitude of confidence and no fear was instinctively understood by the armed protestors. They left without further incident.

Our home in Sturgeon Landing was broken into over the Christmas break though nothing of real value was stolen. It was the first time that either of us had experienced our home being broken into. That experience changed how we looked at living in the village sitting across the river from a First Nation's reserve. The events of violence and threatened violence, though not directed towards us, had created a different kind of tension within us.

During the autumn and early winter of 1976, I put together the research, the interviews, and the photos I had taken and gathered for the Ile-a-la-Crosse social history book. With my wife's help with the typing of the book, Sagitawak: A Bicentennial History of Ile-a-la-Crosse, was finally published.

Our second daughter was born in February. Not long afterwards, the woman who had babysat our first born had attempted to murder my teacher assistant, her sister. We both knew at that point, we had to find a new place to live. With that decision made, we were able to enjoy what remained of the school year in Sturgeon Landing.

We spent the summer of 1977 on the farm where my wife had grown up. We had purchased the house and the home quarter from one of her brothers, and began to plan for the time when we would make the farm house our home. The constant shifting from northern community to northern community began to negatively affect our relationship. She had grown up in this one home, a drastic contrast to my growing up in scattered communities in seven different provinces and going to more than twenty different schools by the time I had finished high school. With the purchase of the home quarter, the tension that had been growing between us eased. We returned to the north for another year of teaching with a more positive attitude. We were certain that we would be back on the farm when the time was right.

The next school year in Buffalo Narrows was another different experience for me. I was not the principal in the large school, nor did I teach high school students. I was assigned to teaching a grade five classroom. Teaching them offered me no real challenges. It felt as though I had been demoted. I had no power nor influence in the school or community. I responded to this situation with silence and a retreat into my own head; and, I began to run. I hadn't run for years, but it seemed that I had to run, and run hard without knowing why.

In school, in the community with our neighbours, and at home, I smiled and pretended that all was as it should be. But, my body had protested and I soon found myself needing chiropractic care for intense back pain. I had long forgotten about meditation and naturism, tools that had helped me in the past. Even writing and photography had been all but abandoned. Only the physical act of running had helped me feel that I was still alive. I pushed my body until I hurt.

As I slipped into depression, with an increasing tenseness growing between us, the decision to have me return to university in order to complete my degree was made. With a degree I would more likely be given a principalship in another northern school. The degree would also make it more likely for me to get a job in the south when it would be time to live on our small farm. With the decision made, I continued to run.

Running had been one of my early escape activities which I had begun to use when I was fourteen years old. I ran to get away from thinking, from being at home, and to escape the abuses that waited for me at home. I had returned to running to escape the image I saw of myself as an unimportant and powerless man, not the strong man I needed to be as a husband and father. I had returned to running and in the process, mirrored the running that was occurring in my professional life – running from community to community, and now running away from the north and teaching to the safety and comfort of being a university student once again. Was I running back to the past, or was I running toward the future? I was doing both. I ran to the past unconsciously not realising why I had run in the past, and I ran toward the future to escape the discomfort and shame of the present. Regardless of why I was running, I was running.

Fourteen months of university classes in Saskatoon followed, non-stop courses through two summers and a normal school year. I took an overload of courses so that I could finish a four-year degree in three years. There was no time for running for exercise. There was no thought of returning to meditation. There were no private spaces for skyclad decompression. While I immersed myself in books and academic life, my wife was left in our rented home in Saskatoon, alone with our two little girls. She was again left on the sidelines.

In the spring, during the final exams for the second term of 1979, my wife's father died. I had already applied for a vice-principal position in a school west of Saskatoon, and I had been offered a choice between two principal positions in the north. However, my wife wanted me to teach in a school that would be closer to her mother's home so that our two little girls could know their grandmother better. My wife had found a school position in a town called Lanigan was less than an hour's drive from her mother's home. The job was to teach French as a second language in the high school.

I panicked as I had stopped learning formal French in grade ten. All I had for French language skills was whatever street French I had picked up while a youth in Ottawa. Yet, the need to please, had me agree to try for the position. I declined the position of vice-principal as well as the northern school principal offers. I was offered the French teacher position in Lanigan. I took the job. Back in the city, I changed my course selection for the spring term in order to take a French immersion course.

Was I still running? I was, only this time, I was running trying to catch up with the changes placed in front of me that were needed to meet my wife's needs for roots and connections. I followed the path being laid out in front of me, hoping that I wouldn't screw up as a French teacher.

Chapter Five

I want to take a few moments here to step outside of telling the story to look at what had just happened. With the deterioration in my confidence, I gave up my authority to my wife. It was as if I had stepped back in time where it was vital to please the person who held the authority over me. It had nothing to do whether the choice was the right choice, it had everything to do with feeling guilty for even considering to continue the career path I had started. Feeling guilty for the distance that had begun to grow as I spent more than a year in university classes, a distance that told me I had betrayed the woman I held as my Magical Other, I accepted the decision to become a French teacher. The Magical Other, with my accepting her authority, she stopped being my Magical Other. It was the beginning of a deterioration in a relationship between equals in love. Love had become conditional.

~

Whatever the reason behind my application to teach in Lanigan, the offer of the job as French teacher in Lanigan made life at home a lot better. We didn't waste any time in buying a house to make into our home. Then we celebrated our new home, we conceived our third child. We sold the farm for the down payment. We were home owners. The house was only three-quarters of an hour from Wynyard where my wife's mother now lived alone. It was close enough to maintain family ties while still giving us our own space. We moved into our home in August, 1979. I began to prepare for teaching a subject I had never thought I would ever teach. It was as if I had just begun a new career.

Before we had barely settled into our new home, my father and his new wife came for a visit. Without realising it, I instinctively returned to the old habit of deferring to him as if I was once again a youth. He had asked to borrow money for car repairs so that he could continue his honeymoon journey. I gave him what I could in spite of my wife's protests. She had told me that I had to think of our small family's needs first. I agreed with her and knew that she was right. However, in spite of that, the little boy within me capitulated.

My experience of teaching in the north made teaching in small-town rural Saskatchewan seem quite easy in comparison. It didn't matter that I was teaching a subject that few of the students wanted to learn. It didn't matter that I didn't have the background knowledge to teach the subject either. Teaching in the north taught me to focus on the students first, rather than putting the subject being taught first. It didn't take long before that strategy paid off just as it had done in the north. It didn't take long for me to convince myself that the move to Lanigan was what I needed both professionally and personally.

Our relationship had begun to return to some normalcy with the familiar environment for my wife. Even the incident with my father soon faded as time passed. Our home was filled with visitors now that we were back in the southern half of the province. Yet, it wasn't somehow perfect. I began to disappear in tiny bits and pieces. But, it wasn't noticeable as I worked hard to please others.

I found myself retreating to watch the others from the sidelines while just engaging enough to avoid appearing to be stuck up or rude. I smiled to cover up some unknown something that was lurking beneath the surface. I didn't know it then, but with my wife's increasing level of comfort, her increased confidence in herself, I lost confidence. My response was to back off. I was in her world, with her family, with her experience that served us so well in this new home. I was in foreign territory living in a home, a real home with a real family where there was stability.

I had no familiarity with roots and commitment to the long run. I didn't have the slightest clue how to do this. I knew that I had to trust my wife to lead us, to show me the way. If it all depended on my leadership and decisions, I believed I would break our family as my father, my grandfather and most of my male relatives had all broken the dreams and plans of the families in which they were in charge.

With the arrival of spring, I returned to running, it was one thing I was good at, confident that I could do well. I had taken on the role of track coach where I coached by example, teaching what I knew as a runner. I was pulled back from the shadows where I had doubted myself, into the adrenalin rush of running where I was in control.

Like magic, in that spring of 1980, our son was born. I was surprised, not so much that we had a son, but that I was now a father to a son. I resolved not to treat him like my father treated me. I was determined to be more present in the life of our family, and within the community. I was "Papa." I wasn't going to be "Dad," as the word belonged to my father. I had to reassure myself that I wouldn't do to my children what he had done to me and my brothers and sisters. I didn't abandon my girls in favour of my son. There was more than enough of me for the three of them and for my wife.

The next seven years passed smoothly, with normal family life. My work was progressing well, and our standing in the community was positive as we had both invested in the community. We extended our participation in the community to fully engage in those activities in which our children were involved. We went camping at every opportunity, alone as a family and at other times with other families.

As part of our camping experiences, we began to skinny dip as a family under the cover of darkness. It was an exhilarating experience that soon came to be shared with our children's friends when they shared the same campgrounds. Under the cover of darkness, there wasn't any shame in being nude.

Nudity in our home was incidental, not planned nor something to be ashamed of when it occurred. We had only one bathroom that had to be shared for bath times. No one freaked out at seeing a parent or a sibling naked. It was simply a natural state in between all the other moments when clothing was worn.

I had resumed university studies with the intention of getting a Bachelor of Arts degree with a major in French not long after we made the move to Lanigan. I had also become an executive member of the provincial French Teachers' Association and had begun to participate in a number of national pilot programs for teaching French as a Second Language. I needed to feel that I was doing the best I could by being as qualified as possible for the roles I was playing. Professionally, my life just seemed to be getting better and better.

In the summer of 1987, I travelled to Ottawa and on to Montreal in order to attend a national workshop. I was to learn the latest methods of French instruction so that I could take part in a national study using the new strategies. I was one of only a few other Saskatchewan teachers chosen for this experience. Being recognised by the provincial and national teacher associations reflected very well on my school and school district. I couldn't ask for more as a teacher.

However, when I boarded the long-distance bus to go to Ottawa, my wife was there at the bus station with our three children, crying as I drove away. Seeing her tears, I felt guilty. I began to believe that anything I did for me, had negative repercussions on my wife and children. I was selfish, no different from my father's selfishness. I rode the bus to Ottawa under a heavy and oppressive cloud of guilt. The weather reflected my mood with electrical storms piercing the darkness, echoing the storms that were swirling within me.

In Ottawa I spent some time with one of my sisters, as well as taking the time to attend a CFL football game with my father. He was in very poor health ill. He had become an in-patient at the veterans' hospital. He was very weak and we didn't manage to stay for the whole game before he had to return to the hospital. I didn't say anything to upset him but rather did my best to give him as much joy in that afternoon we shared together as best I could. I knew it was going to be the last time I saw him. I knew he was dying. There would be no more bi-annual family trips to Ottawa that would include a stop to visit with him, his wife and two stepsons. When I left Ottawa by train for Montreal, I was already beginning to grieve for the loss of my father.

The workshop had taught me quite a few new strategies which I knew would improve my classroom instruction, making lessons more interactive with the students. But the workshop had a dark side that I hadn't counted on. I was alone too much once the workshop activities for the day were completed. I avoided going out with the others for the evenings. I allowed myself to learn, but I couldn't allow myself to enjoy being away from home. In my opinion, it would have been a betrayal, especially when I knew that the socialisation after the days' activities crossed the lines of fidelity for some. I believed that if I stayed away from the after hour's socialisation, I would be even more faithful. I knew too many who weren't faithful when away from home. With this being my first time away from home, I didn't want to risk becoming an unfaithful husband, to be like my father who didn't know the meaning of fidelity.

The evenings and nights were too long, too silent, and too lonely. I talked to my wife every night on the phone while I was in Montreal. Being apart was hard and I could hear and feel the strain of being apart in her voice. I imagined that she heard things in my voice that likely didn't fit with the words I was saying. I wondered if she thought that I was cheating on her. As I listened to her words, something seemed off. As the days passed the conversations became stilted and shorter. I didn't think she trusted me anymore.

The distance that had grown between us while I was in Montreal didn't fully disappear when I returned. We both shrugged it off as we again immersed ourselves into another school year. Besides the usual activities, we had agreed to lead a European trip for my senior French students for the following Easter break. My wife had agreed to be the female chaperone for the trip.

The time until our departure for France in April, 1988 went by quickly with all the work of trying to reformat my teaching instruction to fit with the new methods of teaching a second language. I began having visitors come to the classroom to observe these new methods. My professional status grew stronger both inside and outside of the school and community. With preparing for the France trip, as well as the ordinary everyday stuff of living in a small town on the Canadian prairies, it was necessary to cut back on sleep time, something for which I was grateful.

In the background behind the scenes of this even busier life, I began to have nightmares. Cracks were appearing in my confidence. I was becoming unsure of myself and deferring more and more to my wife's choices in decision-making.

The trip to Europe went well as we guided twenty-five students through France, then Italy, and then into Switzerland. One evening while the students were doing their own thing, my wife and I went down to the Mediterranean Sea in Nice to walk along the shore. With the warmth of the evening air, and seeing a quiet and secluded corner I decided to skinny-dip. It was cold in the water making the adventure a quick in and out experience with the need to hurriedly put my clothing back on because of the cold. It was the first time for skinny-dipping without our children taking part.

Back home in Canada, with the trip completed and with other extra-curricular activities lessening in intensity, I began to slip into a quiet depression. My father died not long after our return in May. I knew something was wrong within me but I didn't know what it was. I didn't seem to be grieving, nor did I find it necessary to attend his funeral. I wrote the depression off as natural grieving in spite of the fact that I had was no feelings whatsoever in relation to my father. I needed to do something different. I felt a hole inside of me that needed filling.

The idea of teaching in Germany caught my eye one day while I was at the university attending one of the last courses I needed for my second degree. I had one more course yet to take the following year and I thought that it would then be a perfect time for us to experience something new, living and working in another country. Initially, the idea was accepted by my wife so I contacted the necessary people to make it happen, including getting permission from the school division, and a letter of recommendation from my current Director of Education. With a plan in place, the inner pressures eased off.

However, with the idea of leaving our home for a year was becoming a certainty, conflict in the form of night storms began to increase in frequency and intensity. She didn't want to go to Germany, didn't want to leave our home and community. Nightmares continued to steal my sleep hours. I blamed myself for my problems with nights. Perhaps if I would have had more energy, there wouldn't have been any night storms. I assumed the blame. Believing that my wife was my Magical Other, a woman whose words contained only truth. So, if there was a problem, I had to be the source of the problem. The night storms that buffeted us were all my fault.

We never talked about those night storms We both sucked in our separate hurts and pains and braved our way through the daytime hours as co-conspirators, united in facing the outer world.

I abandoned the project to teach in Germany and cancelled what had been already done in preparation. I pushed my disappointment deep within me as I withdrew from the program. Then self-talk began to harass me. Did I really want to go? Or, was the plan to teach in Germany about me starting to run again? Was I just being selfish again, uncaring about the needs of my wife?

In withdrawing from the program, I had abandoned belief in myself. The second degree program had finished, there was no year of teaching in Germany in the future, and I was left empty. The degree now seemed meaningless. Nothing was going to change because of the degree. Afraid of the emptiness, I searched for ways to fill that emptiness. I needed something to fill in the holes in my psyche.

And so, I began to plan for a Master's degree in psychology. I needed another series of classes in order to have the undergraduate requirements for a psychology degree. I had the intention of becoming the in-school counsellor for my students and of being in charge of peer counselling. I talked it over with my wife who suspected that I was getting another degree, not for the practical needs of my career, but in order to fill in the holes that had left me living as a zombie.

Falling into another depression had left me without much desire, with little energy, and without a sense of purpose. Being a husband and father wasn't enough. I doubted that I was a very good husband given the many ways that I seemed to be failing as a husband and as a man. My world was turning gray. I suffering from a repression of life.

I need to turn to the words of Carl Jung here to explain, in part, what was going on within me. I was losing my life force, or libido. Normally we think of libido as sexual energy and not as life energy in itself. Jung tells us that libido:

"denotes a desire or impulse which is unchecked by any kind of authority, moral or otherwise. Libido is appetite in its natural state. From the genetic point of view it is bodily needs like hunger, thirst, sleep, and sex, and emotional states or affects, which constitute the essence of libido."[4]

With my body and mind caught in a vicious cycle of denial, with a blockage that refused to release the pent up shadows that haunted my dream world, my body and mind had taken revenge. Libido had been depressed. Dreams had been denied and so had the primacy of my relationship to spouse, family and community. I had become less of a man in my own right, settling for my roles to stand in my place. I went through the motions and worked hard to maintain that illusion to everyone around me, as well as to myself. I tried to convince myself that it wasn't all that bad, and to, "Suck it up! Life goes on!"

I never got around to planning a second trip to France for the spring of 1990. I just didn't have the energy for it. Depressed, I thought a new series of university classes with fill the holes in me and have me stop brooding about my minor problems. I just needed to be busy. The problem was that it didn't really take much energy to do the classes. I was consistently the oldest in all the classes, with the ability to read and retain information without a lot of effort on my part. I did well even though I wasn't giving the courses the attention they deserved.

Repressed libido needs to go somewhere. It wasn't going into my teaching which was becoming automatic rather than mindful, even with the new teaching strategies. It wasn't going into community activities as I was withdrawing into a more passive presence. It wasn't going into our marriage which had begun to suffer because of my lack of libido.

---

[4] Jung, The Concept of Libido, CW 5, par. 194.

Part Two

Descent into Darkness

"A midlife crisis, like an acute neurosis, is characterized by conflict, depression and anxiety."

Daryl Sharp – The Survival Papers

Chapter Six

Jungian psychology uses dreams as a means to access the hidden, inner world of the human psyche. If one looks deep into human history, one finds the power of dreams as they appeared to give voices to the gods and goddesses of ancient times. Dreams play a vital role in shaping to our modern religions through the voices of our prophets. Dreams that are shared find themselves buried in mythology and fairy tales. Dreams show us our deepest secrets, our common bonds across time and cultures. And surprisingly, these collective dreams often expose the core of who we are as a people, as a culture.

When we look at our dreams, we generally find them too absurd to pay much attention to them. Yet, there are dreams that demand and get our attention. Most are nightmares, where the self is somehow threatened, put us into situations of great distress. Some dreams are too realistic for our liking and feel more powerful, perhaps even prophetic for that realism. And some disturb our sense of propriety with scenes of ourselves nude, exposed, vulnerable, and shamed.

~

Over many years I had recorded my own dreams with more than a few showing scenes of nudity, violence, realism, and absurdity. Most of the nudity in my dreams was passive such as finding myself in a public space, exposed, but with no one paying attention. Some of the nudity is found in surreal scenes and magical scenes where all rules are suspended, such as when I find myself swimming deep beneath the surface of a sea with no fear of drowning, or flying naked through the air and through solid mountains as though I was a god. And sometimes, the nudity is sexual with realistic and challenging scenes that shock and awe leaving me wondering if what I had witnessed in my dreams was about my own hidden intentions or desires.

I have also had too many dreams of being brutalised by men, of being devoured by women. War scenes with bloody violence, scenes where I fought darkness and demons in desperate attempts to stay alive, often had me waken with screams and my fists flying out to battle the night monsters both human and imaginary.

In analysis, I told only those dreams that I felt that would get to the heart of my own issues that had sent me into analysis. I was certain that the dreams with nudity had nothing to tell me or my analyst. After all, I wasn't a pervert. I didn't want the analyst to think that I wasn't worthy of being there in the office.

It took me a long while to admit that I had dreams that had me nude. Strangely, it was only after I began to paint some of my dreams that I began to realise that there wasn't anything immoral or intrinsically wrong about the nudity in my dreams. There were important messages for me. But that came years later. In 1990 my dreams were almost indistinguishable from nightmares

> *... sleeping ... dreaming of sleeping in a bed that is only a mattress on the floor beside M ... both of us asleep ... I reach for her and see that she is someone else ... a young woman unclothed with her back to me in peaceful sleep ... I cuddle close holding her close to my chest ... skin against skin but knowing that I cannot enter her ... the pent up tide within me crests and I tighten into a ball as the semen empties onto the bed ... the bed is now a bunkbed, the upper bed, and I am alone ... M is standing looking up at me ... the house has disappeared and is now a small apartment ... I am alone ... then a raucous noise fills the air and I see a line of nude men, surreal men, cartoon men with hard features of the face – square chins and big-mouthed grins ... the men march in time up an escalator going nowhere, lockstep, arm swinging ... their other arm is occupied as their right hands hold proudly forward erect penises ... these men are mostly black ... one winks and grins foolishly and whoops as he ejaculates ... again I'm in the apartment with M ... she is leaving me, abandoning me ... I grab her to shake her and protest ... then I wake up (real-time).*

Libido, repressed libido showed up over and over again in my dreams. Though she appears in the dream, the dream was not about my wife or of my relationship to her. The dream was about libido and its loss. The people in dreams are representing things about oneself that need to be recognised. The dream was giving me a warning that I didn't hear. I pushed it back, denied it had any worth or meaning. What is repressed will find its way out to confront us in the outer world.

Jung wrote in a book called <u>Aion</u>:

> *"The psychological rule says that when an inner situation is not made conscious, it happens outside, as fate. That is to say, when the individual remains undivided and does not become conscious of his inner opposite, the world must perforce act out the conflict and be torn into opposing halves."*[5]

But what was it in me that was being repressed? What had tied up all of my energy, my libido? I could and did blame so many in my world, sometimes blaming them unfairly, some with reason. But mostly, I blamed myself.

I began to think that I needed someone or something that would allow me to regain a sense of balance and well-being. I was set adrift in a sea of victimhood without knowing that I was a victim or why I was a victim. My past had been wiped out of my mind. Nothing made sense when the life I was living had everything a man could ever ask for. I had it all, a loving wife, great children, a good career, and a community that respected me. Yet, there I was, sinking into darkness and despair.

At that time, I was embroiled in conflicts with all who held real or imagined authority over me. Of course, I didn't know it at that time. I believed that my school administrator was deliberately making my life miserable. He had noticed the changes in me and expressed doubts of my ability to be an effective student counsellor and denied me the opportunity to take on the leadership of the peer-counselling group. In my mind we became enemies in spite of all the support he

[5] Jung, Aion, CW 9ii

had shown me over the eleven years I had been working with him. In spite of what I thought, he continued to support the twists and turns that arose in my classes that now included the role of computers in the classroom.

The conflict spread into the community. I had been co-coaching for a number of years but that had changed. I had willingly taken on the role of team manager because of my need to invest more time in my university courses. Yet in spite of that being my choice, I began to resent the two other men who filled in as coaches, somehow believing that I had been ousted as not fit to be one of the coaches for the team.

Most damaging, the conflict had crept into my relationship with my wife. As my depression worsened, I had somehow abandoned the responsibility for most decisions to her. I didn't have the energy nor the will to make decisions. I didn't have the energy for the give and take that went into negotiating decisions. It was simply easier just to accept what she wanted, when she wanted it. I believed that she, my Magical Other, would make all the right choices which I would then support. However, the more I abdicated my responsibility and the more she was forced to step up and make necessary choices, the more resentful I became. I became angry, a repressed anger that I would then swallow so as to somehow keep the peace in our house.

Again, the face of libido being repressed did its dirty work by seeping out. I want to turn again to Jung for an explanation of the repression I was experiencing, a repression that had me internalise my anger and then unfairly project that anger onto others.

> *"Repression, as we have seen, is not directed solely against sexuality. Bit against the instincts in general, which are the vital foundations, the laws governing all life. The regression caused by repressing the instincts always leads back to the psychic past, and consequently to the phase of childhood where the decisive factors appear to be, and sometimes actually are, the parents."[6]*

---

[6] Jung, The Origin of the Hero, CW 5

As I write these words twenty-five years after that period of time, I can see that the trigger of my father's death, which had not allowed me to address painful questions about my childhood, was in part what lay behind my regression from a mature, adult male into a brooding shadow of a man. I was on a downward spiral and was burning bridges behind me. In the process, my Magical Other had somehow transformed into the Dark Queen, and I was afraid of her. Little could I have guessed that to be included in the decisive factors of my childhood were events that would centre on my mother, and that my wife's shadow evoked the shadow of my mother who lurked in the darkness ready to devour me. But that, was a story that wouldn't come to my awareness until twenty years into the future.

Why was this happening to me at that time? Was it just because my father had died, a man who had abused his authority of father leaving me desperate to please him simply to stay alive? The answer was 'yes, maybe'. Yes, his death served to awaken something in me that had been bound away, denied, and then forgotten for the most part since I had left home to become a man. Maybe, because there were things in my current life in which men with authority were unconsciously complicit, dealing with their own issues of power and authority. These were only some of the questions that went unasked. I had entered into an in-between world, into midlife. I had begun to suffer a midlife crisis.

Another dream at that time surfaced and warned me, but I paid it no attention thinking it was just another in a long line of nightmares.

> "... I'm in a house with death ... the house has a hole that is trapezoidal in shape, a hole about the size of an eye, a rough edged hole ... you can see the light from the inside looking at the whole ... inside in one room there is a dead man ... I think I'm responsible for his death in some way ... some other people are also in the house ... I have a sense that one of them will soon be dead ... it's dark outside ..."

Who were these people in my dream? I didn't recognise any of them. Did they represent people I knew in real life? In spite of my efforts, the contents of the dream made no sense, so I abandoned the dream though it never did abandon me. For whatever reason, the dream had been written down by me in one of my early journals, one of the few that survived the years. I knew that dreams were important, that if read right, there were answers to questions to be discovered.

Chapter Seven

Loss of soul. The loss of libido, the loss of one's life force and energy is the loss of soul. Most forms of psychology and psychotherapy have no room for soul. The word is too wrapped up in religious dogma. My studies of psychology led me into a place in which I had once wandered as a youth, the world of depth psychology and philosophy. In those areas, the ancient idea of soul was still alive and well.

It is hard to believe in the existence of something, anything, until that something disappears and leaves one with a sense of loss. We feel the loss as a feeling of emptiness. This is probably the truest for soul. For most people, the soul is a religious concept that one accepts without question, or rejects. Anyone who is not a "believer" generally accepts that the soul is simply a delusion, a figment created by religions to have people ignore the bad things happening to them and to those around them. Yet, there comes a point when some people, in spite of their religion or their lack of belief, search for answers that resonate with more than just what the head, what their ego tells them.

Perhaps, it has to do with the fact that the word soul has become too broad and as such, almost meaningless in the process. Carl Jung suggested that a more relevant term, anima, which is a Latin term that means 'the vital principal of life,' would allow us to look at and understand loss of soul, a state of being which leaves a human shrivelled like a raisin, a shell of a person, following a midlife crisis.

> *"The anima is not the soul in the dogmatic sense, not an anima rationalis, which is a philosophical conception, but a natural archetype that satisfactorily sums up all the statements of the unconscious of the primitive mind, of the history of language and religion . . . It is always the a priori element in moods, reactions, impulses, and whatever else is spontaneous in psychic life."[7]*

---

[7] Jung, Archetypes of the Collective Unconscious, CW 9i

Depth psychology goes on to explain that all we understand as soul, is projected onto others, particularly others who are of the opposite gender. For me, that projection of soul was placed on my wife, something that comes with 'love at first sight.' When in the presence of someone upon whom we have projected our soul, we feel alive, animated. All is well in the world. However, when the projection of soul is withdrawn, something that isn't necessarily a conscious choice or decision, one falls into a depressive state of soul loss. For so many, midlife is that unsettling time of life when all the knowns that have served as the foundations upon which we have built our lives and our belief systems, have come crashing down. We suffer loss of meaning, loss of libido, loss of soul.

I, like so many others, had felt my world beginning to fall apart. Yet, when I looked at my outer world, everything was going on as it had always gone on. The outer world was oblivious of the panic and fear that raged within me. I didn't know it at that time, but I had been given the "call" to take back ownership of my soul. The life path I had been following had hit a crossroads. Which way would I turn? Would I follow that call or turn and run?

It didn't feel like a journey that I wanted to take. All I could feel was that I was losing everything I had treasured and worked so hard to achieve. I feared what would be found within myself if I dug too deep. I believed that whatever existed in the past, needed to remain hidden. The past was too dark, filled with too many ghosts, and was not a good place. Of course I didn't consciously know that this was what was going on within me at that time. All I knew was that my certainties had come tumbling down. And so I scrambled for escape routes in order to avoid that approaching darkness within me.

> *"There is no coming to consciousness without pain. People will do anything, no matter how absurd, in order to avoid facing their own Soul. One does not become enlightened by imagining figures of light, but by making the darkness conscious."*[8]

---

[8] Jung, Psychology and Alchemy, CW 12

I didn't want any more pain. I had more than my fair share of pain. I had worked hard to escape the poverty I had lived within while growing up. I worked hard to have a family and had become a respected member of a community. What was I to do? My Magical Other had become a fallible human in my eyes, no longer a goddess on a pedestal. That was an unbearable loss. There was nothing inside of me to hold onto without her holding the light that would take me through life. In spite of her becoming a flawed human, like me; I refused to allow her to be less than a goddess. She was holding my soul. However, she was suffering her own pain with little energy or will to be the caretaker of my soul.

My wife was faced with losses as well. The man she had married had effectively disappeared leaving a stranger in his place, a man who cowered in dark corners, unsure of himself, and unable to make decisions. Yet, in spite of all that, she held on to me as I held on to her. We both held on tightly to our marriage, unwilling to admit defeat. The focus for both of us was our children, our extended family, our engagement to the community, and our careers.

But there remained for me at least, a need, an unbearable need to reconnect with my soul in spite of the fact that it had been projected onto the woman I had married.

Chapter Eight

The school trip to France, in 1991 was done alone as I didn't have enough students going to pay for a second chaperone. I felt relief in spite of the emptiness I felt in my gut. I have little recall of that trip. Yet, from the perspective of the students, it was a good trip. With the return back to school, the junior students were anxious to begin organising their own trip for the 1993 Easter break. Our first daughter was going to be a part of that group. I worked consciously, together with her and my wife to create a good experience. I had something concrete in the outer world to focus upon and it helped keep the shadows and the hungry ghosts of the past quiet.

I continued on with my studies in psychology at the university. I filled in the hours of my days as much as I could. It was enough. The next year and a half passed without serious emotional issues. My work at school and my participation in the community returned to a somewhat normal state. With our united focus on things other than our relationship, we somehow dodged the blows that could have destroyed our marriage at that time when we were most vulnerable. Life was as good as it could be given the darkness that bubbled uneasily beneath the surfaces.

In the early summer of 1992, I entered into a Master's in Education program with the focus on Instructional Technology. I had thought I was going to register for the Educational Psychology program but a new Master of Education program caught my attention. I got caught up in the idea that I could be a world leader in the field of distance education using computer technology.

The decision to abandon the psychology degree wasn't based on logic. I was distracted by novelty. Likely, my psyche wasn't ready to be immersed into the world of psychology. With a new focus, and now an Internet account which I could access from my home using a modem connected to my telephone line, I entered into the new world of Computer-Mediated Communication. All of a sudden, I felt a surge of energy, a return of libido. I connected with people who challenged the world as it was. There were no judgments by others based on normal outer world status indicators; we accepted each other through our presence created by our words that appeared on the computer screen. Judgment was reserved for what one said, the ideas that emerged in dialogue. I became more visible through my words, and more respected for ideas that I felt that I could never speak of within the confines of my face-to-face world. I grew in confidence as I mingled with others who had doctorates, others who were authors, and others who had the respect of so many in their personal face-to-face worlds. With them, I became an equal.

There was a danger in my immersion into the world of cyberspace, the danger of becoming even more disconnected in my daily outer-world life. The more energy I invested in being present in cyberspace communications, the less energy I had for being present in my everyday life as a parent, teacher, coach and husband. I didn't know about Internet addiction. It didn't even exist at that point in time as few peope had any access to the Internet in the days before the World Wide Web. I simply assumed that my constant connection to this inner world was because of my educational goals. Regardless of my thoughts, I was addicted to engaging with spirit at in cyberspace. My soul had found a different place in which to be projected.

In spite of the unknown dangers of Internet addiction, I did discover treasure in my efforts with Computer-Mediated Communication [CMC]. I brought my communications modem to school which I then connected to a school computer using a very long telephone line. I engaged my students in experimental dialogues with other second-language students in other parts of the world. My conversations with others built a network upon which I drew in order to enhance the classroom experiences for my students. Though most in the community didn't understand much about the computer or about the Internet, I was seen as a wise person, an explorer of sorts who brought back treasure for my students and the community.

The next two years passed with fewer night storms in our marriage. We had both immersed ourselves in our areas of passionate interest. We gave our best efforts to our work, our community, and ourselves as individuals as best we could. If anyone would have looked in on us from the outside, they would have believed that we had it all. Did we believe it? Did I believe it? Those are questions we rarely looked at, though we both knew that there was trouble brewing beneath the surface that we didn't want to talk about.

By 1994 I had shifted my focus from CMC and second-language teaching, to exploring the possibility for psychotherapy and counselling in cyberspace. It seemed to be the perfect environment for psychology and making a difference for the world. I was drawn into this alter-universe as I pushed myself to explore ideas in depth and even wrote poetry in attempts to allow the truth of who I was to be set free. And, there were responses to my words in cyberspace.

Without realising what had been taking place, I had opened the portal to the collective unconscious. What appeared in my poetry and in dialogues in cyberspace was the voice of my soul projected onto others who heard echoes of their own soul. I had simply cast my soul free into the ether of cyberspace. It was as if I had cast a handful of tiny hooks into an ocean with no real intention or expectation of catching any fish. The projections were cast out, and there were others in cyberspace who heard the voice behind the poems, others who believed they had found their missing soulmate, their Magical Other, reflected in those words.

I didn't hear the desire in their voices that responded to my posts, it was as if I was deaf. I heard my own voice being heard. I became fascinated by my voice. With every resonance heard in the responses of others, my self-esteem blossomed. I began to think that when I reached high enough I would find myself as a pure soul, a Buddha-like being, a wise saint-like presence. I became almost a guru for those who were caught in my web of words. The problem only got worse as I was caught in my own web of words.

In the world of cyberspace, projection flies freely, especially when all that is used to communicate are the words spoken and heard. We each create our unique and personal version of the other voices. Each created an image of the Other responding to their words. There are no scars, no imperfections that marked these Others. I sensed, at least on a subconscious level, that I was somehow cheating on my wife, not in a physical sense, but at a much deeper level which had her stripped of "magic" which was then placed on others who were more illusion that real people. I had placed the magic belonging to her on the images of Others created in my mind. My connection to soul was withdrawn from her and projected into a digital space.

And so, our connection as a couple weakened. What had held our marriage together through all of this, had been our unified commitment to our children, as well as a deep-rooted stubbornness that didn't allow us to take the easy way out. We both retreated into a silent truce while wearing forced smiles in public and in front of our children. We rarely admitted to each other, even in the middle of night storms, that something was poisoning our marriage. We fought about the surface conditions of our life together, quiet fights so that our children would not hear us in the middle of the night.

Another trip to France took place during the Easter breaks of 1993 and 1995. The trip in 1993, went well with our first child. It was the perfect way to end her high school studies before heading off to college.

Our second daughter and her classmates were set to go during the Easter break of 1995. Like the other trips, it was a success for the students. Unlike other trips, my lack of energy created an extra sense of freedom for the students. I found myself struggling more than usual when we returned from the 1995 trip. Because of the growing unrest in my marriage, and my addiction to the Internet, I had a struggle keeping my head together. I was finding it harder and harder to hold onto my sanity. My work at school was deteriorating and my level of commitment as a coach was fading though I refused to give up on being coach for my school teams. As a result, the quality of my coaching disappeared and with that, the commitment to my athletes. If I hadn't had a strong reputation as a coach, I am sure that I would have found myself without athletes to coach.

The Internet addiction continued to make it worse. I had taken leadership roles in two online discussion groups and had joined several others which focused on online psychology and counselling at distance. I soon found myself engaged in counselling others on-line. There was one woman who was a relatively famous singer in the U.S.A. who somehow became a person I counselled. She suffered from severe depression and was suicidal. Over a period of several months, a bond of trust was created between us. The trust deepened the counselling relationship.

One evening, she divulged a plan to commit suicide, a plan that would have had her sacrifice herself as a bloody offering on an altar in a church in which she was to perform. She intended to perform the act of sacrifice the night after her performance. In a panic, I got her to give me an emergency contact number as well as a promise to call me before she tried to follow up on the plan. It wasn't too many hours later when the phone woke me with her crying, alerting me she was indeed going to complete the sacrifice. She just couldn't take living anymore. She hung up before I could say more. I immediately called her contact and told him of the plan.

She was apprehended at the church by the contact person who took medical help with him. He was aware of the potential for her committing suicide. Following my advice he took her to the hospital where she would be treated and protected. It was months later that I heard again from her. She was both angry and relieved. She was angry that I had betrayed her by having her committed to a psych ward in a hospital. And, she was relieved that somehow, the care she got there had returned her will to continue living.

We both realised that what had happened with the counselling and the intervention based on the Internet dialogue, was something important. Her need for on-line counselling had come to an end. She now had a face-to-face therapist who worked with her. The on-line counselling had been born, and I was one of those who pioneered in the field of practicing mental-health counselling on-line.

Back in my day-to-day world, my edges were fraying even more. A younger female teacher who I had once considered as a France trip replacement for my wife when she initially refused to go with me, began to appear in my dreams. Those dreams ridiculed me, laughed at my attempts at keeping a safe distance from her. My wife heard her name spoken in my tortured sleep. And again trust was broken.

I realised that I desperately needed help. In a state of panic, I reached out to connect with a teachers' federation counselling service. I had hoped that making this effort to engage in counselling as a client rather than as a counsellor would make my life change for the better, that it would in some way, fix me.

Chapter Nine

I began counselling with a man who looked more like a lumberjack than a mental health professional in the late spring of 1995. Over the remainder of the school year, I had managed to calm down enough to successfully navigate the hurdles in my work as a teacher. However, I had begun to see my life so bleakly that I had considered suicide, something I had not considered since my teenage years in Ottawa. The turn to being counselled saved my life.

I made it through the rest of the school year and hoped that a summer break would make all the difference in being more balanced for the next school year.

Yet, the world of cyberspace claimed more and more of my energy and attention. I became more and more sensitive to the slightest hints of criticism from the people around me at work and in the community. I retreated into my computer room with curtains drawn to hide the light.

My wife feared for my life as I dropped deeper and deeper into depression and irrational behaviours. I had begun to beat myself up with fists flying into my face. I raged whenever I felt the slightest criticism. My anger burst out with words punctuated with punches that I knew hurt her emotionally as much as they hurt me physically. She learned to tread carefully around me fearing that I would go too far in my rages. In spite of our both retreating into quiet corners, the night storms increased in frequency and intensity. There were too many issues. As I began to spill out secrets of my childhood which began to ooze out telling me stories of my being abused as a child. I was again becoming suicidal.

Summer turned into fall only to find that I was almost incapable of managing my way through a day of teaching. The only part of the day that seemed to give me relief was the engagement of my classes with other French as a second-language classes through the Internet. In the world of Computer-Mediated Communication, I was the expert, I was the undisputed authority.

It didn't take long into the school year for me to again call my counsellor in a state of panic. A few more counselling sessions later, he was convinced that I was spiralling downward rather than learning coping skills. It wasn't just a simple problem of teacher burnout from over-extending myself. There were deeper issues that were being touched and needed to be dealt with.

Just as the cross-country running season was drawing to a close, I knew that if I didn't do something drastic, I wouldn't last much longer. The darkness was becoming overwhelming. My counsellor rushed to have me included in a therapy retreat with other teachers who had found themselves unable to go on teaching. The retreat was to begin on the last day of the running season. I arranged to have another teacher take my students home from the cross-country competition. I left, following the last race, to drive to the retreat site.

Normally I am a man who drives at the speed limit or just slightly below that limit. I often got teased about my rigid adherence to the speed limits. Yet, that afternoon, I found myself driving as fast as I could, often hitting in excess of 150 kilometres per hour on the rough country roads. As I drove, at times I thought of veering off the road to intentionally crash into a telephone pole, or to swerve into the path of an oncoming large farm truck. Perhaps it was cowardice though I told myself it was because of the pain and shame that my suicide would inflict on my children that kept me on the road. So I drove on, pushing as fast as I could, to reach the retreat centre on the shores of Lake Diefenbaker.

There was no need for me to rush, to drive like a madman as that first evening was simply for registration. Few of the retreat staff had arrived by the time I got to the site. After settling into my room, I took out my journal, a new book I had purchased just days before, along with a set of coloured pens. I began to tell in writing to myself why I was there. It felt like a religious experience as I wrote with great care. With the first words recorded, I left my room and slipped out of the building to wander through the trees along the edge of the lake. I wasn't ready to meet others who were arriving and settling into their small rooms.

I wasn't the only one who had the same idea. I saw a woman standing at the edge of the lake, so I took care to move further down the shore. I felt I needed the distance. I just didn't feel like socializing.

We met as a group later in the evening at which time we were given the rules for the weeklong retreat: no caffeine and no liaisons between the participants. We were introduced to the leaders of the retreat which included my counsellor. His presence served as an anchor for me. The work of the retreat was set to begin in earnest the next morning following a group breakfast. When the group was dismissed, I went outside to be alone rather than mingle with the others.

One of the other counsellors at the retreat went through the process of teaching us about the use of meditation as part of the healing process. The work we were doing at the retreat was teaching each of us the skills that were to help us help ourselves on the journey of healing. We meditated together three times each day. Music played in the background as we were guided to places of safety in our minds. Structured group sessions followed, therapy sessions that were intent on teaching us behavioural strategies for navigating safely through our dark moments.

One of the activities had us take turns standing alone within a circle and then placing others within our circle representing those closest to us from within the group. When it was my turn, I had all the others in the group enter into my circle, and then I left the circle to stand outside the group. For some reason, during the first part, everyone was feeling good about being placed within the circle, but that changed to shock when I left the circle. I couldn't explain what had happened when pressed. In the process, I had created a dissonance in the group which had worked so hard at trying to be inclusive while also trying to be honest. I had settled for total honesty without consciously realising that I had evoked darkness with the dissonance.

I cried a lot during the retreat, always at night away from the presence of the others. When in group sessions or at meals I reverted to my pleasant and considerate persona, a pleasing persona. If anyone had been observing, there would have been no indication that I was in need of counselling. I tried everything that was asked of me, though usually finding my response constrained and passive. I was a person encased in medieval armour and nothing seemed to pierce that protective barrier.

And, late at night, I would find a quiet corner, away from others. I huddled in the darkness, holding my knees to my chest, and cried silently. The repressed libido had to go somewhere. When I was finally exhausted I would retreat back into my private room and write in my journal before finally falling into a fitful sleep filled with strange dreams.

By the time the retreat was done, I had somehow released most of the pent up tensions that had me attend the retreat. I was able to return home and go back to work a lot more functional than when I had left. I had discovered helpful strategies that would help me maintain the gains I had made. I returned to meditation, something I had abandoned somewhere along the way. I felt good about what I had learned. I felt hopeful that I would finally be able to pull myself back together.

Yet, with the return home, I realised that I had left a trail of broken hopes and fears behind me at home and in the community. The ripples that followed in the wake of my needing to go to the retreat had affected my family, as well as others who knew me as a friend and colleague. My breakdown had shocked them, leaving them unsure of just how to deal with me on my return.

I was able to navigate through the rest of the first semester, through Christmas and the New Year without another crisis. I had begun to hope again that I had gotten through the worst part of the haunting darkness that had plagued me. I believed I was only going to get better and stronger going forward into the future. The worst was now safely behind me.

Our first born daughter, got married not long into the new year. Life was very good. I was a very proud father of this beautiful young woman at the beginning of 1996.

Chapter Ten

In early 1996, as with every other school year, it was time for a teachers' convention. Conventions were a diversion for the most part with us getting more out of being released from teaching for two days, than from the content of the seminars and presentations which we attended. However, that year it was different. I attended a session led by Kelly Walker called "Soul Loss", a session that examined what happened when a person suffered burnout. I wasn't prepared for what I heard:

> *"Midlife is a time for new awakenings. Crisis. Yes. Awakening to the TRUTH often causes us to abandon hitherto valid life scripts in honour of new truth. What a pity that this often causes deep wounds in those around us. Perhaps that is why we ought to go to the desert for period of time. Alone."*

Midlife. I found something in that word that was like a lifejacket. I continued to listen to Kelly Walker, sitting on the edge of my chair. I realised that what I was hearing was vital to my well-being and my own journey.

> *"It is soul loss that happens when the good, generous and often very successful, in most aspects of life, women and men begin to fall apart from the inside out. Generally it is the outer shell that is the last to break down. The inner breakdown has been going on for some time before it appears."*

I wrote furiously as the presentation went on. Almost everything he talked about described what had been happening to me. I had been suffering soul loss, a midlife crisis. I left the conference more energized than I had felt for years. I rushed home with the intention to study more and find more answers about the issue of midlife crisis. Of course I hadn't heard or understood everything he had said. Some things you can't hear because you're not ready to hear them.

Back home I found a book called, The Survival Papers: Anatomy of a Midlife Crisis, by Daryl Sharp, a Jungian analyst. His book led me to other books by other Jungian analysts. I was flying high, certain that these books held all the answers that I needed, and with their knowledge I would be freed from the depression that was intent on bringing me down. As a bonus, I could then use what I learned to help others as a counsellor.

That high began to fade fast. Knowledge wasn't the real issue. In my rush to understand, I had somehow bypassed the words quoted by Daryl Sharp in the introduction to his first chapter: *"When an inner situation is not made conscious, it happens outside as fate."* There was too much I didn't know, stuff hidden and denied from the past, and until that was dealt with, I would continue to suffer as a victim of my past, blaming fate, blaming others.

In spite of the discovery of books by Daryl Sharp and James Hollis, and the convention presentation by Kelly Walker, I had work to do in my life outside of my preoccupation with midlife issues. I had a book chapter to finish and my last half class to complete before the end of the school year. Digging deeper into Jungian psychology would have to wait. But even more distracting, was the draw into cyberspace, a world on the other side of my computer screen where I was all that I dreamt I could be. The separation between physical reality and a virtual reality had become blurred to the point that there was no separation.

In spite of all my efforts to focus on my last half class, the chapter for the online education book, and my resolution to get my act together as a teacher, I continued to invest too much of my energy in cyberspace. I spread myself thin with multi-tasking so that there was little hope that anything could be done well. Regardless of my fractured attention span, I finished the last course and I finished the chapter of the book I had committed to doing. I then began to work on my thesis. It was a work that would finally allow me to steer my own course in life.

I brought together all I had learned from both my classroom experiments with on-line communication and from my engagement with various on-line discussion groups. I presented my global plan to the man in charge of my thesis committee and he rejected the plan. He didn't want a thesis that didn't involve a lot of testing data. His version of a successful thesis was a quantitative, statistic-riddled study. He encouraged me to forget about writing a thesis and to do a project instead.

I was left shaken and discouraged. I knew that I had to have this man's approval if the thesis was to ever be accepted. I didn't consider his suggestion of re-approaching the Master of Education degree through the project route. I went back to my classes with a series of questionnaires for my students to complete so that the data from the questionnaires could become the statistical component of the thesis. I gathered the data grudgingly. I wondered how I could possibly blend those statistics into the qualitative approach that formed the foundation of my thesis. The anger that began to grow within me was the fuel that allowed me to complete the school year without incident. The thesis and my advisor was the enemy.

While this was going on in my academic life, I had decided to invest in becoming a better qualified track coach with a focus on middle and long distance training. I had met an Olympian at the training centre who I convinced to bring a team of other Olympians to give a series of weekend workshops to my high school, so that all areas of track and field would be represented. Though a few of the skills introduced were not on the high school competition schedule such as hammer throw or race walking, all the disciplines were covered. My students thrived on the hard work demanded of these coaches.

In the summer of 1996 I had been asked to be one of the coaches for the zone track and field competitions. Those competitions would qualify athletes for the following summer's Jeux de Canada Games to be held in Brandon, Manitoba. I was able to persuade a few of my school athletes to take part in the event. All those who had placed well in the school district competition and at provincial completion were automatically given invitations to the Zone competitions.

I added three others to the team to represent our zone in the race walk and hammer throw competitions. The top two finishers in each event would go on to compete at the national games the following summer, the Jeux de Canada Games.

My race walk competitors both qualified, the female athlete winning her event and the male athlete who was my son, getting the silver medal. At the provincial team selection meeting for the Jeux de Canada Games, there was a suggestion to not include race walking athletes as the races were significantly shorter than at the national games. I argued for their inclusion following a qualifying trial at full distance to be held the next weekend. If any of the four athletes who had competed at the summer games could complete the distance with a respectable time, they would be included on the team for nationals.

Only three of the four took part in the competition with both my female and male athletes being part of that group. Only my son finished without being disqualified while posting a provincial record for the five kilometre juvenile event, a record he broke while finishing the full ten kilometres. It was enough to have him included for competition at the Jeux de Canada Games the next summer and had him ranked in the top ten in the country. I was proud of him for his efforts, not only because I was his coach, but because I was his father.

I finished the school year with a firm belief that the future was now turning out for the better – I was going to finish my Master's degree, my son was going to compete at Nationals, my reputation as a coach was spreading, and I was seen and recognised as an expert in the world of computers and the Internet. And, perhaps more importantly, we were going to celebrate our twenty-fifth wedding anniversary later in the summer.

Once the school year was done, I was given an office to use for the summer at the university. I could work uninterrupted whenever I made the trip to the city. It wasn't long before I took my sleeping bag to the office so that I could spend a few nights there saving money through reduced driving expenses. It gave me enough alone time to finish the thesis. I had other professors who were long-time friends, read the thesis before I presented it to the chairperson of my committee. The other professors assured me I had written a solid thesis. I was ecstatic.

However, he wasn't satisfied. He again suggested that I write it up as a project rather than a thesis, with even more focus on statistics. He told me to bring the project to him the following year after doing a few more studies with more statistical analysis of those experiments. I returned home discouraged. There was still time left in the summer to work through the thesis again giving more importance to the statistics I had gathered without losing the thesis. I believed that in the end, he would accept my work as well done, in thesis form.

I began to spend more and more time at the university, finding it increasingly difficult to make the long drive back to my home as I struggled with the task. At least, that is what I told myself and my wife. I began to think that I needed to drastically change my life in order to escape the growing darkness and depression. I searched for and found a studio suite near the university and began to think that perhaps I could find work at the university as a lecturer and enter a PhD program once I had finished the thesis.

With nothing more than these vague ideas in my head for the future, I wrote my wife a letter telling her that I wanted out of our marriage, that I wasn't good enough for her and that she would be so much better off with me out of her life. Somehow I had come to believe that she would be relieved to get rid of me. But when I gave her the letter and saw her cry in response to it, I knew that I had lied to myself and her. She still loved me. She still wanted me in her life.

I knew that I couldn't go back to work on the thesis anymore, as my life was at home and in my community. When I told the Dean of Education of my intentions to settle for Post Graduate Diploma, he tried to talk me out of it. He had read my thesis and knew that it was almost ready for publication. He suggested that I reconsider. He told me that I could get a new chairperson for my committee, a man who was both qualified and a friend. I refused. I was done and I knew it. I submitted the necessary forms for the PGD and for convocation. I returned home feeling defeated and ashamed at having failed my dream. All that held me together was knowing that my wife still loved me and still wanted me in her life.

And then, in that summer of 1996, I became a grandfather for the first time. The miracle of being a grandfather to a grandson, the day before my forty-seventh birthday, vowed to do what I could to honour my marriage and my family.

Chapter Eleven

The week before classes were to start in August, 1996, my wife phoned me to get ready to help her at an accident scene. I had been a volunteer ambulance driver and attendant for the ambulance service she operated. Our son was one of three injured in a car rollover. I shifted into Emergency Response mode as I helped at the accident site. It took two ambulances to get the three teenagers to hospital in Saskatoon. It wasn't until the ambulances drove away with my wife monitoring our son and another in her ambulance that I found myself shaken to the core.

Our middle child had been in a roll-over the year before, late at night, an accident that didn't require ambulance service. I had responded to her call home for help. At that time, I had also been shaken though thankful that she didn't need hospitalisation or treatment. My son was in serious jeopardy. He had been the driver and was the most seriously injured. The car was totalled. I saw the damage and I blamed myself. If only I had been home that summer, he wouldn't have been . . .

I couldn't go home and be there alone. I returned to the school and buried myself in busy work. I didn't want to be alone as I would think too much. I shuffled back from the book storage room to my classroom with books for my students, a task that didn't demand much from me. Later, when I was in the copy room preparing my documents for opening week, various teachers stopped to ask how I was doing and what I had heard from my wife. Everyone was supportive. I needed them, these teachers who I had almost abandoned. The realisation that these people were important to me, gave me something to lean on at that moment. Hearing their words, I was pulled back from a very dark place. A few days later, we celebrated our twenty-fifth anniversary with these same people, our friends at the school. We had reason to celebrate. Our son was going to be okay.

Over the next several months, life returned to some sort of quiet normal. There were no university classes to claim my time so I focused more on strengthening my counselling skills. I worked to include more Gestalt strategies, as well as adding in Solution-

Focused Therapy techniques following a training workshop. I increased my participation in the provincial association for counselling becoming a member at large on the executive committee. I read as many books as I could about Jungian psychology. I had begun to think again that perhaps I would become a Jungian analyst when my teaching career was over, perhaps even sooner.

In spite of my efforts, I again began to slip into depression. My dreams became tortured. I felt as though I had entered a swampland and was caught in murky slime that was drawing me down into its depths. Trying to escape these nightmares, I would walk out into winter snowstorms to curl myself into a ball in an empty field not far from our home. I would hold myself tightly as I could, as though that holding would prevent the pieces breaking apart and scattering in the snow by the storm raging outside. A street lamp was the only light visible in the cold and dangerous darkness.

Christmas

In the depths of a winter's night
I wandered alone and discouraged
Lost without soul or hope
I found myself alone even in crowds
A world of reaching arms
Filled with raucous voices
Yet, a silent world
Even within the noise.

There, in the depths of that night
I noticed a thread of light,
A beam that touched and lit
My heart and soul. And I,
Nervous on this winter's night,
Stood within a field filled with
Christmas song and hymn,
A field of starlit mystery

There, in the heart of winter
I sang a prophetic hymn

Of a man, a woman, and their child.
I found myself cradled

I had been writing poetry in both English and French for more than a year. The poetry betrayed the desperation I felt in my self-imposed isolation. I had lost all respect for myself and felt abandoned. I felt the distance between myself and the rest of the world grow. I knew that if others saw me, really saw me as I was beneath the charades I had been living, they would flee from me. The poetry I had written told the story of a man in search of Eros, a search that projected Eros onto others both in my day-to-day life and my life in cyberspace.

I had shared most of the poems with my wife in with hopes that she would see the passion that belonged to her and that she would pull me back into life, into a renewal of our own love story. But it needed more, it would take more than words to bridge the canyons that separated us. Just before Christmas, I put the poems into a booklet which I gave to her as a gift, and then I gave copies to all of the staff at the school. I wondered what they would think, what they would say about the gift, about the poems. I was surprised at the positive response. All but one teacher acknowledged appreciation.

That one teacher had returned the book of poems to my mailbox. I had personalised the books, so I knew who was rejecting the gift. It was the woman upon whom I had years earlier projected Eros. Of course, my wife knew about my confused relationship with this teacher, a non-physical relationship. The fact that she appeared to evoke response through my unconscious projections in nightmares and my irrational responses to this teacher, I was guilty of cheating on some level. The weight of that guilt was added to the rest of my self-hatred issues.

In early 1997, one of my brothers committed suicide. Hearing that news, I buried myself in my office at home and I cried for him, for myself. I sang a song to him called, "Go Rest High On That Mountain." Then, I fell apart. It didn't make any sense to me as I had not become depressed with the deaths of either of my grandparents or my father. Yet, in spite of the fact that I hadn't seen much of my brother since I left home more than twenty-five years earlier, and had no communication with him for the past twelve years, I was undone.

For the next few weeks I went through my days on autopilot. I turned to my new counsellor, for help as my previous counsellor was unavailable. I still had my son's trip to France to plan and his competition at the National Games in the summer to follow. These two tasks became my anchors in the outer world. I knew that I needed something for an immediate focus, not so distant into the future. I began a series of at-distance courses for counselling certification.

I turned again to the Internet and became part of a new group for online counsellors. I then set up my local counselling practice as an official business. It was a genuine and intentional immersion into a new direction for me, but it was also a much needed distraction and diversion. My work as a counsellor, and the courses, used enough of my time and focus to let me hold myself together.

The trip to France during the Easter break of 1997 went better than I had hoped. In spite of the demand for more trips, I had no personal stake in digging deep within me to meet that demand. I was burnt out.

The end of the school year in June, 1997 was a shambles. I found it necessary to invent marks for my students. I had had no energy to legitimately mark projects or give many tests during the semester. I found myself giving old exams to the students to prepare for the final. I hoped that somehow I had actually taught them the material that was being tested. When it was time for final exams, I was so unprepared that I found myself photocopying old exams just hours before the exam was given. In spite of the unprofessional acts of inventing marks, no one seemed to notice. The students were satisfied with their marks. The school administration was satisfied as well.

It was only my role of father and coach that kept me from falling apart and giving in to the darkness.

Father

He is father, this stranger who walks bent under
unknown weights shouldering unknown sufferings.
A man's eyes tell of his separateness, his aloneness.
His remoteness leaves me feeling lost, feeling less.

He is father, this man who sits quietly at the table
who sits listening to the voices of a family.
A man's silences tell of his journeys to fearful places
speak of his doubts, his sufferings, his needs.
His silence leaves me feeling abandoned, alone.

He is father, this man.

I spent a good part of the summer of 1997 with my son, training him as a race walker. He was getting very good and I pushed him to be even better. At the Jeux de Canada Games, he finished fifth, with a personal best time. He was the youngest athlete in the competition. His strong showing in the race had been noticed and he was asked to take part in the Pan-American Games. He refused. Race walking was my passion, not his, and he knew it. He taught me a vital lesson in standing up for himself, one that I would have to duplicate only months later.

With a new school year ahead, we took in a Mexican student into our home so that our son would have a new friend, a brother of sorts. It was his last year of high school and we hoped that we could make it his best year.

I began the 1997-1998 school year began with renewed high expectations. I vowed to be more professional in my work with year plans, semester plans and course plans created to guide my work. I vowed to keep my teacher's daily journal up to date and to ensure that I had good and reliable data for evaluation purposes for my students. My ability to hold to those vows crumbled before the arrival of winter.

With the end of the cross-country season came I became desperate for help, calling my previous counsellor who was now available again, looking for extra counselling sessions. I felt my efforts at school beginning to fail in spite of my intentions. He soon realised that I needed to have more help than he could give me.

My intuition told me that I needed to begin working a Jungian analyst. However, the closest analysts were living and working in Calgary, a seven hour drive from my home. I gathered the information for entering into analysis thinking that with the end of the school year I could begin psychotherapy with one of the analysts. All I had to do was to somehow survive until the end of the school year. I hoped that two months of analysis would be enough to shift the depression enough so that I could become a more functional teacher and husband when the 1998-1999 school year began.

In October 1997, I wrote:
I am here

I am here ...
caught between night dreams
and the world of day
eyes ringed with sleep
again disturbed

I am here ...
in this netherland of
current and cursor
eyes tracking
the flow of words

I am here ...
stuck

My best efforts to regain mental control were failing. I soon found myself again huddled in the darkness, in my home office. I lost myself in tears and to fear. The night storms between us had increased in frequency leaving us both battered and afraid. I found myself behaving erratically in both the school and the community. I wandered down back lanes at nights wanting to avoid the street lights. I needed the darkness where I could hide. I became obsessed with imagined terrors and dark immoral longings. I was paranoid about the school administrator and the new Director of Education believing that both were working hard to have me resign as a teacher in the school. I was resentful of my son's hockey coaches, feeling they had pushed me out of a meaningful role on the team. And then there was the issue of the female teacher who had returned my booklet of poetry the year before. She was always there on the sidelines. I was drawn like a moth is drawn too close to the light of a fire. There was no escape.

I began to avoid entering the staff room when this teacher was there. I was certain that she hated me as she left the staff room whenever I had to enter the room. We didn't talk to each other, not even to say hello. I didn't desire her as a woman, but that didn't matter, just the sight of her set off strident alarms within me. I feared the teacher; yet was caught as though I was being drawn into in a spider's web where I would be devoured. And that fear was attached to the gut fear that was buried deep within me kindled by my mother, whom the teacher resembled in body type and facial structure.

As the winter approached, I dreaded seeing this teacher walk down the hallway passed my classroom. I became more and more hyper-aware of her presence in the school. She returned to haunt me in my dreams, laughing at me, taunting me as she engaged in twisted sexual acts with other male teachers. It was as if she was determined to show me what I was missing in not choosing her over my wife. My fear refused to listen to reason.

The night before the last day of classes before the Christmas break, a night storm left me with bruised cheeks and black eyes. I punched myself over and over again while I defended myself against the words that were assaulting me. I only stopped lashing out when I had finally exhausted myself. I was in deep trouble and I knew I wouldn't be able to finish the school year. It would be lucky if I would be able to finish the semester.

I hid my bruises behind sunglasses that last day at school before Christmas. I was thankful that I would have two weeks to recover, for the bruises to heal, and allow me to gather my strength for the rest of the school year.

On Christmas morning, while the house was silent as the first light appeared in the back yard, I was in my home office feeling as far from festive as one could possibly feel. Looking out the window into the back yard, I found words to capture the feeling, a poem written at that time only in French:

Matin silent, matin de Noël

Pas de bruit ce matin / It is silent this morning
Sauf pour un vent leger / Except for a soft breeze
Qui fait danser ... / That stirs
Sauf pour une horloge / Except for the clock
Qui fait voler ... / Marking the fleeing of time

Regarde par la fenêtre / Looking through the window
Pas de neige / No snow greets the eyes
Seulement la terre endormie / Only the earth sleeping
Pas d'enfants / No children either
Seulement la balançoire démunie / Only the swing swaying

Regarde dans le salon / Looking into the living room
Un arbre garni de lumière / A tree decorated with lights
Un symbole visuel / Stands as a symbol
Un espoir promis et mystère / A symbol of hope and promise
Ce matin de Noël / This Christmas morning

Somehow, I had hope in spite of the overwhelming sense of loneliness. Our last child was still at home and he had turned into a young man. Too soon there would be no distractions focused on our children to distract us from having to deal with our issues. I would then be forced to confront myself and face what was happening to our relationship. The showdown was approaching; only, it would come sooner than I wanted or would have predicted.

Chapter Twelve

It wasn't long after classes began following the Christmas break when I found myself again in a desperate panic with the approaching semester exams and the need to find marks for my students. My wife was alarmed with what she saw as I scrambled with last minute tests which turned out to be copies of previous final exams. She asked our family doctor to meet with me after telling him what was going on.

I made another appointment with my counsellor and drove off to the city for an evening appointment in the second week back in classes. He was surprised at how much I had regressed following the last time I had seen him. He listened as I talked and cried my way through the hour. At the end of our session, he gave me a task, to begin writing my story. Journaling was a task I had given to some of my clients and so I was familiar with what was expected and why this was so important. Why had I not already done this? I was to give him what I had written for our next session set for a week later.

For the first time in my life, I deliberately sat down to confront the past, my past. I was done running from it, at least that is what I tried to convince myself. Whatever ghosts from the past were chasing me needed me to stand my ground and face them head on. Over the next few days, the words poured out of me. I wrote at home, and I wrote in my classes while the students worked through past exams in preparation for their final exams. I had my students mark each other's exams and then I recorded them in my book. Finally, I would have some data to use. When it was time to return to my counsellor's office, I had thirty-seven pages of remembered history ready to give to him.

Our session had me talk about some of those remembered abuses, I had suffered as a child, recorded in the journal. I spoke about the physical abuse I received from the hands of my father, and about the chaotic changing of schools and addresses across different provinces. There were hints that there was much more to be remembered. Yet, for the moment, it was all I could cope with as my story as it had been remembered. The counsellor remarked at the end of our session that I needed to work with someone who could work at depth. Taking that first step, the pressure within me eased and I was able to complete the semester without further mishap. I began to hope again that I could make it to the end of the school year.

As the February break approached, I again felt the pieces falling apart. Bits and pieces of my past were emerging from the shadows where they had hidden, challenging me. I was coming undone, I couldn't face going back to school with the sewage of the past appearing. I remembered an incident of being sexually molested by my grandfather. With that remembrance, a Pandora's Box of other sexual abuses by other adults in my life had begun to open. It wasn't just about physical and emotional abuse or dissociation anymore. My dreams became charged with sexual energy that had me as a witness rather than as a participant. I went again to my local doctor to see if he knew a psychologist that could perhaps help me as I couldn't wait for summer and access to a Jungian analyst.

The doctor sent me to a psychiatrist he had heard of in the city. The psychiatrist responded with anger as I told her about my problems. She scolded and told me to go back to work and stop looking for an excuse to get medical leave. I was stunned and frantic. A quick call to my counsellor got me an emergency session with him. Between the counsellor, my doctor, and my wife, it was decided that I couldn't delay beginning intense psychotherapy. I made calls to Calgary and got interview appointments arranged with the two analysts who were working in the city for the following Saturday.

In Lanigan, my doctor wrote out a report for the school division indicating that I was going on medical leave for mental-health issues. The director of education protested the doctor's decision and said he wanted me to get a different doctor's opinion, one that he would contact. It was hard to replace a second-language teacher and a computer teacher, let alone a teacher who could teach both disciplines.

I refused to agree to see another doctor believing that my doctor's statement was more than enough to meet legal requirements. Seeing that I wasn't going to back down and that he would have no choice but to accept Tom's medical statement, the Director told me that I was to leave the school without telling the staff why I was leaving. Mental-health issues needed to be kept as quiet as possible so that the staff wouldn't be upset. Before the school administration could act to stop me, I called a staff meeting and told my colleagues why I was going to be gone; what had happened to me; and what I knew about my past that needed to be resolved.

I tried to call a student assembly follow up that meeting but that was immediately blocked by the principal and the Director who had arrived to get me out of the building. So, at my wife's suggestion, I turned to the local newspaper to tell my story to the students and the community. I let them know that I was going to be gone from the community and why I needed to leave. I didn't want rumour to run rampant. This community deserved the truth. Though I was going to be gone for mental help, my wife and son were remaining in the community and would need the community's support.

The school principal and the director were angry that I had gone around them directly to the community. The director told me in anger that I wouldn't be returning to teach in his school anymore, that teachers who burnt out never came back. I had burnt my bridges. At that point, I didn't care. I just needed to get help. Neither the Director nor the principal had been in Lanigan long enough to understand the depth of connection that existed between the community and the teachers who had committed to being in their school for the long haul. I owed the community, and I needed that community to be there for me and my family through the tough time that was yet to come.

My wife drove me to the city and I met with ZM, and MS, the two analysts I had previously contacted. While I was in interviews, my wife found me a place to live, a room in a co-op house within walking distance of MS's office. The location of the house helped me decide which of the two analysts I was going to choose. With the choice made, she had me buy a laptop computer so that I could leave our desktop computer at home for her to use. The analytical sessions were set to begin the first week of March.

For the next six months I attended three sessions per week with MS, focusing on my dreams and using art therapy to help me regain psychological balance. I attended evening seminars and week-end workshops in addition. I wanted to get a better grasp of my situation from a Jungian psychology perspective. It became a six-month period of full-time self-rescue work. On the side, I joined in a Jungian psychology on-line discussion group which was in process of falling apart.

It wasn't long before my dreams began to let me know that what I was doing was working, that I was moving in the right direction in confronting the darkness and the dangers buried deep within me. A dream from my first week in analysis affirmed the risk:

> *... the baby boy is in danger of falling under the wheels of the train ... I try moving forward to save him from certain death but I lose sight of the boy ... the driver of the LRT sees what is happening, me trying to rescue the boy and the boy slipping towards the wheels ... he begins the slowdown of the LRT ... I feel terrible feeling unable to rescue the boy ... it appears too late to save him as he has disappeared ... the LRT has stopped and I rush forward and to my amazement find the boy safe ... with a whoop I quickly pick him up, hug him, and give him a kiss ...*

I had learned years earlier that all of the people in dreams are all different faces of the self. I was the little boy, the driver, and the ego who works at trying to rescue the little boy. I was rescuing the inner child who had been abused by parents, other adults, and by a life of chaos.

But it wasn't all positive. There were many, too many dark shadows that threatened. I was getting more and more exhausted and wanted to quit the whole process. It wasn't long before I found myself crying for no apparent reason: crying in the middle of the night when sleep refused to come; crying while attempting to write my story or while writing the dreams I remembered; crying in the middle of the afternoon when I had the house to myself; and crying on my drives to and from my home in Lanigan, every second weekend. It didn't feel like I was getting any better. Intellectually, I knew that this was part of letting go of the ghosts of my past that had been called back from the banished corners of my psyche. I was crying for the boy who didn't have a protector.

As I worked with my analyst over the late winter and spring, it felt as if I was going over and over again, the same stories with changes that didn't seem to lead anywhere significant. One of my dreams from the end of March highlighted this:

> *... I am wandering down nature trails searching for a particular path ... searching ... I find the river after crossing sand hills, dunes with bits of grass ... I cross the river using things floating in the river as a raft of sorts*
> *... I find myself back where I had begun the search and again set off on the quest ... again and again but each time there are variations ... I find myself back in time though still in my present state of age and awareness ... I see a house, part of row-housing ... I'm inside of the house and sense the poverty ... it's small, dark, and in disarray ... it's old and in need of repair ...*
>
> *... I find myself in the arms of a young woman ... I am caressing her and wanting to possess her sexually ... my hands are under her clothes, touching her skin and sparking a fire of desire within me, a lusting ... she is forbidden fruit and I know it ... I've been here before ... I ache to enter her here in this messy place of poverty ...*

The dream was a dark dream for me. The idea of *forbidden fruit* made me wonder what it was from the past that had evoked this part of the dream. I understood the idea of finding myself back where I started from which the dream was telling me, a message that I didn't heed as I continued to try and stay one step ahead of my analyst. I didn't realise that *forbidden fruit* was going to become a significant part of my healing journey fourteen years later.

My ego wasn't as powerful as I had thought. MS was a needed guide as I tried to navigate through my inner swamplands. With her guidance, I was able to reclaim most of my life, more than enough to seriously think about returning to a normal life as a teacher and as a husband.

Just as I began to reclaim that life, I became a grandfather for the second time to another grandson. My wife and I met in our daughter's home to celebrate that new life. Again, as I had with the birth of my first grandson, I felt a renewed commitment to outer life. It was as though another candle had been lit in the darkness.

By the beginning of summer, I decided, with the help of my analyst that I could go back to work in the fall. I let the school know, and the rest of the summer was focused on making this happen. With that planned, another plan was put into place for continuing analysis with MS every second weekend. I had a plan, a goal and with that, I was able to move forward as a man who had regained control of his world.

Chapter Thirteen

In the fall of 1998 I returned to teaching in the high school. I was more functional as a teacher than I had been for quite a few years. Making the drive to analysis, allowed me to keep that hard won balance which I had worked so hard to achieve. It wasn't easy to return to the same school and community, especially after exposing my past to that community. It wasn't easy, but it was a vital part of my recovery process.

My greatest challenge was working with the school administration and the Director of Education. Neither of them wanted me back in the school, especially after I had taken control of my exit from the school in order to go for analysis. In spite of their lack of support, I had the support of most of the staff which made all the difference. These were the people who had been there for me when I was falling into depression, who had been there for my wife when I found myself doing analytic work in Calgary. They were my friends as much as they were colleagues.

In March, 1999, my analyst, had heard enough of my constant complaints about the principal and the Director. She challenged me to do something about it, to become the authority rather than complain about it from a safe distance. I had been in the school and the community for twenty years and had only another six years to go to retirement. To jeopardise my career, and to abandon this community for a new one in which I could be the school administrator, was not a decision I could take lightly.

The relationship with the Director deteriorated. He was making it harder for me, as well as the school principal who was realising that I was not broken any longer. I was doing a good job teaching. He apologised to me for contributing to the problem rather than giving me support when I had needed it. Yet, is spite of that apology, he continued to follow the directives of the Director who wanted me gone from the school. Fed up, and still angry about how the principal had unfairly treated our Mexican "son," while I was in Calgary, I took the challenge given to me by my analyst, and decided to apply for a position of principal rather than stay and complain about the principal and Director in Lanigan. It didn't take long for me to find a school that hired me in as a principal, an immersion school in Zenon Park, Saskatchewan. It felt good to be recognised as worthy of being their new principal, yet it didn't feel so good to be abandoning the town that had been my home for twenty years.

Getting the job was the easiest part. The hardest part was making the transition from teacher in Lanigan with a family, to living alone in another community where I would be the principal in a different school system. My wife had invested too much in the community to give it all up without my proving that I could actually do the job and stick with it. She had been worried that the pressure would only result in me having another mental crash. I commuted between the two towns at least twice a week for the school year of 1999-2000. At times, my wife would make the commute to Zenon Park in order to spend time there with me. She needed to see for herself how I was doing in the school and community. She also needed to figure out if she would fit into that French community should I continue to be principal there the next year.

The challenge went well and I was valued as the school principal by the community, the Director, and by the other administrators in the school district. The only negatives that emerged were my environmental allergies which had worsened, and the fact that the francophone portion of the community was unfriendly to my wife who didn't speak any French. Knowing that she wouldn't be able to fit into the French community, and concerned about how my allergies had worsened, she decided that staying in Zenon Park wasn't going to happen. If we were going to be together for the following year, I would have to find a different school in a different community.

And so I began another job search. I found a job as principal in Canwood, a larger school in an English-speaking community. Because of few housing options available in the small town, we bought a house in Shellbrook, a larger community that was less than a half hour away on a very good highway. We made the move early in July, 2000.

It wasn't an easy move, especially for my wife who had to give up her community roles and her career. In spite of the losses, being together was more important for both of us. We had spent half a year apart while I was in Calgary, and a full school year apart in the last three years. Neither of us did well when we were separated.

Before the end of the summer, things began to deteriorate at the new school, even before the school year was ready to begin. The Director who had hired me, had found a new job and his replacement was a former classmate of mine from university. We hadn't been friends at university where I had consistently earned higher marks than him. In spite of my having met with all the teachers and having created a teaching plan based on their preferences, someone had stirred up the teachers to protest their teaching assignments, the same assignments that they had asked for in our interviews together. The Director wouldn't listen to my explanations. He supported the teachers' demands regardless of the evidence I offered to him.

Unknown to me, I had walked into a minefield where key members of the staff had joined together to lead a revolt against my being the principal of their school. Another person in the district had tried for the job. He was a friend of those key teachers, a principal in a smaller nearby school. The teachers, at least the core group who ran the school, wanted him as their principal.

While problems at the school and with the new Director began to unfold before the start of the school year, our second child chose to get married in a civil ceremony in our new home. She had chosen a man that made her smile and that was all we needed to know. Not knowing how the drama with the teachers was unfolding in the background shadows, the September long week-end wedding was a real celebration for us. We were glad that our second daughter was marrying a man that she loved and who loved her in return.

It wasn't long into the year when things worsened at the school. Teachers, with the full support of the Director, worked constantly to have me be taken out of my position. Innuendo and vague complaints were treated as facts that needed to be dealt with and fixed by me. Not knowing what was really going on behind the scenes, I was left to struggle with the situation as best I could. I focused on administrating the school, working with the First Nations community that had been threatening to remove their students from the school.

The parents and elders from the nearby reserve met with me and decided to keep their students in the school. That decision meant that we could then keep all of our teaching staff and not lose any budget as well. A major problem had been solved, especially since I had been told to redo the teaching assignments assuming the loss of those students. Since I had admitted to being Métis, and having joined the local Métis association, an additional level of distrust was leveled at me by the Director.

For the first time in my teaching career, students began to be overtly disrespectful to me. I began to doubt myself and tried harder to build bridges with them. In the community where I lived, Shellbrook, it was a different story. Both of us soon found ourselves with friends. My wife had found work in her field, working at the nursing home and at the hospital. I had become an executive member of the local Métis society. For the first time, I no longer felt the need to hide my indigenous roots. We golfed together and made more friends there as well. The contrast between the community in which I worked and the community in which I lived was like night and day.

In early winter, a formal enquiry was launched by the Teachers Federation in order to deal with the complaints they had received about me from the teachers. The Director had agreed that a formal enquiry was needed. The complaints were treated with seriousness because of the numbers of people laying the complaints, complaints supported by the Director. I learned that I was insensitive to all staff members, and it was suggested that I was sexually inappropriate with the female staff members. No specific examples could be brought forward to substantiate any of the complaints which made the enquiry difficult for the representatives of the Teachers Federation. All that could be proven was that the atmosphere was toxic.

The mere suggestion of my potentially being a sexual threat to a few of the female teachers without any specifics brought forward to substantiate the vague complaints, had raced through the community. I was judged as guilty even if there weren't any specific acts of sexual misconduct for which I was being accused. I realised that I was effectively done as a principal in the school. I informed the Director that I was immediately taking stress leave because I couldn't combat the culture of slander in the school and community. Not realising the politics operating in the background, the District Board of Education put pressure on the Director to fix the problem he had created. The Division Board had seen what I had done to save the school enrolment and staff numbers and they had been impressed. Instead of going on stress leave to finish the school year, I was given the role of principal in Shell Lake.

The four months in the Canwood School had broken my confidence as a teacher with twenty-five years of teaching success. It had broken my confidence as a principal in spite of my early career successes and the experience of the previous year in Zenon Park. I had four and a half years to go until retirement, and that self-confidence would never return. Of course, I didn't know that at the time. I assumed that all would be well again once I was in a different school.

I swapped schools with the principal of Shell Lake, the man who had been the choice of the Canwood staff. After an initial period of distrust in Shell Lake, I soon found myself working well with staff and students, and the local board. It was a small school and I began to think that it would be the perfect place to finish my career.

Yet, in spite of what was going on in the school, the Director told me that I wouldn't be in the school the following year as no one wanted me there, nor in the school division. My local school board was surprised and dismayed when I informed them of my search for another school principalship as they thought we had developed a good working relationship together. They were unaware of the Director's comments. The local board hadn't heard any complaints from the staff members or from the community. The Director simply wanted me gone. He did offer a good recommendation for my search for a new position.

Chapter Fourteen

I was fortunate to find another school in a different school division that had need of a principal. The next stop for me was in Mortlach. I was told by the Director who hired me to clean up the school, to get the teaching staff back on track. There was a culture of relying on student suspensions to maintain control that needed to be fixed. He had fired the last principal against the wishes of the staff. My real job was to create a culture of respect in the school.

I had doubts about the job not long after taking the job, especially when I found out that I was once again facing a hostile staff and a hostile community. The only reason I took the job was my belief that in this situation I had the full backing and protection of the Director of Education as well as that of the Division School Board. What I hadn't counted on was how I had been overly sensitised, especially with regards to women, something that would make my work in the school more difficult. I was slipping too much into trying to please them rather than confront them for their bad behaviours. I didn't trust them enough to ever meet with any of them while alone in my office which they sensed. They saw my weakness and they exploited it.

The house we moved into was a teacherage provided by the school division. The school was directly across the street from the teacherage, a beautiful, modern building. The student enrolment was higher than in my previous school, which meant that I would be getting a higher salary. The community itself was set in the middle of a dusty plain with busy railroad tracks running through it. The house shook with every train that passed. I was about as far from being at home geographically as I could get. We had always lived near trees and hills and water.

My colleagues administrating other schools in the district, were an ambitious and energetic group of principals and vice-principals. I soon became part of the technology team which the Director wanted to use to build the reputation of the division. His vision was to have us be the most technologically advanced school division in the province, if not in the whole of western Canada. I found myself thriving in this culture of technological excellence. But, in the background, a different and darker story was beginning to unfold. I was under attack, an attack that was also targeting the Director.

We soon found out that whatever was discussed in my office was heard and communicated to the school staff and to the community. The Director had me relocate my office so that it didn't have a wall shared by the secretary's office which was open to all staff members. Staff and community had quickly engaged lawyers to challenge our right to be administrators. I was fortunate to have the district school board on side and actively speaking on my behalf to the local school board.

In the background, the previous principal, now a Director in a different school division, was a significant player behind the scenes, of the vocal and powerful opposition to both the Director and to myself.

While this was going on, I worked with the students to begin building a level of mutual respect. They were the first to notice that they weren't being unfairly punished. Before I disciplined, I listened and took what I heard into consideration. I mediated and counselled when appropriate. Under the previous administration, it was the school versus the students, the students who were not the children of the community leaders.

Student suspensions were drastically reduced. Although there were still too many suspensions. From the community and staff points of view, there were drastically too few suspensions. They believed the school was an unsafe environment. In an effort to help change their mindset, I took a role in teaching as I knew that this was important for both students and teachers. They needed to see the principal as one of them rather than being a person out of touch and apart from them.

The problem students became less and less of a problem and soon more than a few of them were in my office for informal counselling. The parents of these 'problem' students became my advocates in the community as they felt their children weren't unfairly being targeted anymore. My confidence as a teacher returned. But, it stopped there.

A small portion of the community had asked the Teachers' Federation to revoke my teaching license. This group was composed mainly of the family members of those few teachers openly challenging my presence in the school. They were hoping that impending legal action would somehow make it impossible for me to ever teach again. Their primary objective was to get rid of me and the Director. I knew that another part of the community was supportive of me, including the town's mayor who had become a friend.

With this knowledge, I deliberately decided to do the work of rebuilding the school culture using a Jungian approach with the approval of the Director. I brought the book, The Hero's Journey: How Educators Can Transform Schools, to structure the approach I would use to change the culture of the school.

I brought the staff together for a two-day workshop in order to hammer out a mission statement and a belief statement for the school. We needed to collectively shape and own the school's guiding principles. A powerful set of documents emerged which were voted upon and accepted, mostly because they ended up being their words based on what they wanted for the school. In spite of the result, the staff felt manipulated into making these very public statements about what was needed for a positive school culture. The intensity of their rebellion via their families and friends escalated.

Before winter had fully set in, an external group was brought in to evaluate the situation. After numerous questionnaires and interview, their findings proved that there was an orchestrated collusion to destroy both myself and the Director as administrators. They realised through extensive interviews with the staff, students and a significant portion of the community, that the campaign had begun before my arrival in the community and that what I did or didn't do while at the school was irrelevant to the plan. The Director was furious and encouraged me to charge forward with the project to reform the school, even if it meant the removal of a few key staff members.

For Christmas, we travelled to Jamestown, North Dakota, to see our third grandson who had been born the week before Christmas to our second daughter. We were now an international family.

By the time spring arrived, one teacher had been fired and another teacher had been transferred. More changes for the following school year were promised by the Director.

Over the second half of the year there were fewer student suspensions. There was movement, real change, but not enough to have me feel confident enough to want to stay and endure more of this concerted opposition. I was the bad cop and now the school needed a good cop, at least that was my opinion. I felt I needed to move on to a new school with the Director's reluctant blessing. I hadn't yet figured it out, but I wasn't ever going to be comfortable as the authority figure in a school. I just was not capable of dealing with the politics of a community school. I believed in playing by rules of fairness, something that was making me too easy of a target for those who had no qualms about getting their way without regard to fairness or rules. For them all that mattered was their agendas.

Chapter Fifteen

It was with relief that I found a new school in Elrose, an older school that was vibrant and positive, with fewer problems. I had thought I had gone to apply for the principal position of the Eston School, but soon found out that the man who had been principal in Elrose, was being moved to Eston by the Director. My wife and I had already toured the community of Eston a week earlier. We liked what we saw. She would have been able to become an ambulance worker again with shifts as a Special Care Aide in the nursing home between ambulance runs. For her it would be a return to the career she left in Lanigan. I accepted the position as principal in Elrose in spite of the fact that I hadn't done any advanced gathering of information about the community in preparation for that position. I accepted their offer because we had both wanted out of Mortlach.

My fear of being alone with a female staff member continued to influence my relationships with the new staff. I was careful, very careful in talking with the female staff members. I would always have my vice-principal, a woman, sit in on all such meetings. It became apparent quickly, that the staff was basically satisfied with me as their principal.

Having been burnt in the previous schools, I began to wonder when my professional life would begin falling apart in this new school. Would I make it through the year? Would I be able to make it through the next three years in order to retire? I was in no rush to buy a house even though I had managed to sell the house we had bought in Shellbrook before we moved from Mortlach. I needed to prove to both my wife and myself that I could stay in the school and the community.

In the fall of 2002, I began my tenure as principal in Elrose. My wife joined the local volunteer ambulance association. The year went well, a lot better than I had expected. There were problems of course, as there are always problems in a school where teachers and students and parents end up in assorted conflicts. Most of the issues were minor and easily resolved. What was different about the school in Elrose was the belief by students and staff that education was important and that respect was the best way to get that education.

The students worked hard and played hard. Most of the teachers had no reservations about putting in the extra time needed for coaching, leading student activities, and tutoring. Perhaps most important in the process was the belief of the community in their school. In a way, it was as if I had found the twin school to match the school in Lanigan.

At the start of our second year in Elrose, with everything going well, we decided to buy the house we had been renting. There had been no indications that I was going to begin having problems that were political. We had both made friends in the community. And, we were grandparents to our fourth grandson, the second child for our daughter in North Dakota.

Near the end of my second year, the decision for my tenure was being considered, I was led to believe by the Director in early May that all was well and that I would be receiving confirmation of my tenure in the school as principal before the end of the school year. I had read his final report and it was only a matter of the Division Board meeting to ratify the Director's decision. Then, before that meeting, it all began to fall apart.

I had to call in the Teachers' Federation because of a serious set of allegations by a few female students against a male teacher who was new to the school. Things moved so fast behind the scenes that I was caught by surprise when less than a week later, the Teachers Federation supported his dismissal, something that rarely happens. Before he left, the teacher visited me at my home and told me that he had been told that I was next on the chopping block, that I had serious enemies. My days as principal were numbered. I assumed that his words were nothing but bitterness about my not being able to protect him. But, it turned out that he had spoken the truth.

The next Division Board meeting resulted in them not accepting the Director's report and demanding that I be placed on a strict one-year extended probation with a wide variety of areas of concern being raised, areas that had not been noted in the report he had given the board. The Director retired and a new Director took his place, a man I knew well and had considered a friend. I believed that with his support things were going to turn out much better. But, it didn't turn out that way. Behind the scenes politics ruled, especially with a new Director having no experience in the role and fearing his own job loss if he didn't follow what he was told to do.

In that third year in December, 2004, I was told that I would not be able to continue as principal in the school, or as a principal at another school in the division for the 2005-2006 school year. In spite of months left to address issues, the decision had been made. If I refused to resign my position, I would be demoted to a teaching position at a different school in the division.

I was devastated. I couldn't understand what had happened. The local school board, the community, and my staff had supported me and respected me and were as confused and upset as I was. Every voice I heard told me that the school was running better than it had for quite some time. It was only at this time that the pieces began to fall into place letting me know that it was politics that were forcing the issue for reasons that had nothing to do with me.

We went to Cuba for the two-week Christmas break in 2004. We both knew that this was the end of my educational career. I was defeated and without the will power to search for yet another school to hire me as their principal. I had wanted to remain in education for at least another five years, in this particular school and community. Elrose had been adopted as our home community. I felt a deep sense of shame for having failed to make that dream become a reality.

The nightmares that had vanished not long after my analysis in Calgary in 1998, returned while we were in Cuba. A mixture of alcohol, a deep sense of failure, and self-blame saw me return to physical and mental self-abuse. We both feared what was happening to me.

In the daylight hours, I found myself inexplicably stripping off my clothes and sunbathing on the balcony of our suite at the resort in Cuba. I had never dared this much nudity since the early years of our marriage other than our long standing tradition of night-time skinny dipping escapades, a family affair. Neither of us risked confronting my nudity.

My wife was just as upset as I was about the turn of events in my career. I wasn't sure if she was upset with me or with what had happened to me. However, it wasn't long into the Caribbean vacation when I learned that it was both.

The re-emergence of nudity in my life was an unconscious response to pressing shadows within. I would once again need the healing powers of the sun to be strong enough to make the journey through the darkness and the storms that were coming.

Once school started up following the Christmas break, I gave my notice to the school board for my official retirement. It was enough that I had completed thirty years in public education. I was finished with the politics of administration in public education. I was in dark place with no dreams for what was ahead for me. I had no sense of what was to happen next in the spring of 2005 as I put in the last few months of my career in the community school. I had no ambition.

Part Three

Swamplands of the Soul

"An old saying has it that religion is for those who are afraid of going to Hell; spirituality is for those who have been there. Unless we are able to look at the existential discrepancy between what we long for and what we experience, we will remain forever in flight, or denial, or think of ourselves as victims, sour and mean-spirited to ourselves and others."

James Hollis, Swamplands of the Soul: New Life in Dismal Places

Chapter Sixteen

What was I going to do now? I refused to give up on the community of Elrose which we had adopted as our home. We had good friends and a home which we had been improving and reshaping to be our home. I wasn't sure what was going to happen next, but whatever it was, we were going to keep our home. There would be no running away in shame. My wife suggested that I could return to work in a northern school. Since I didn't have to worry about money anymore, all I needed was something to do that would make me feel good about myself, something that would give me a sense of purpose. With my experience and education, she reasoned, that I needed involvement in a school.

In April, 2005 before the end of my last school year in Elrose, I applied for and was given the job of principal and Director of Education for a reserve school not far from my first school in the far north of the province. In early May, I was flown into Fond du Lac to meet with the Chief and the staff of the school that were to remain for the next school year. I gave each person a separate and private interview hoping to learn what they needed and wanted for going forward. In a strange way, it was like coming home as I met a former student of my first school in Camsell Portage. He was the son of my first teacher assistant. First impressions were very, very favourable.

It didn't take long for me to once again become involved in an intense political storm. The staff was fearful of the idea that the principal would also be their evaluator. They wanted someone else to be Director, to do teacher evaluations, someone at a safe distance. The Chief refused to listen to their complaints and encouraged me to do what was necessary to transform the school into a place that was less violent and more accountable. He had me double check the teaching credentials of all the teachers which led to the removal of a Special Education teacher who had no teacher training nor a university degree. The teacher I hired in replacement was qualified which did a lot to ease the tension that had been growing between myself and the rest of the staff.

In spite of the tensions among the teaching staff, everything else appeared to be going well, especially in terms of my relations with the band council and the chief. I was doing the necessary work to make their vision for education on the reserve become realised. I attended formal meetings of the band council, as well as of the Prince Albert Grand Council (PAGC). The relationship with the Federal government was on the verge of solving critical issues on reserves, especially in education. Expectations were high throughout the fall and into the beginning of winter 2005, because of the proposed legislation that was aimed at fixing much of the Indian Act.

In October, my wife flew off to North Dakota for the birth of our fifth grandson while I kept busy with meetings and administration. At Christmas time, I got to meet the latest of my grandsons when all of our children and grandchildren came home to Elrose for a reunion. In spite of the challenges of life on the reserve, life and work appeared to be on track.

Following the Christmas break, towards the end of January, the mood on the reserve took a sharp turn. All the work at the PAGC with the Federal government looked to have been wasted for it appeared that there was going to be a change in government and leader who had a drastically different philosophy in dealing with First Nations issues. The local council lost faith in the Chief and began to agitate for personal agendas which only served to divide the community. The Chief didn't have the power in this climate of conflict to continue driving his vision for the school and community.

A charge of harassment was levelled by a young, white female teacher against another teacher who was First Nations. I listened to both sides and found myself trying to protect the young teacher who was terrified and ready to quit because of her fear. It quickly became a racial issue rather than a harassment issue. On the advice of the Chief, I put the male teacher on paid leave until the matter could be resolved. At a band council hearing that was investigating the charges of harassment by the male teacher, I was told to reinstate the male teacher and told to be careful about which side I chose to support as it could end up very bad for me. The meeting ended with my being told to stay in my teacherage while the committee considered what should be done. In effect, I was put under house arrest by the committee.

I left that meeting after being threatened by a few of the councillors. It was a reserve with a violent history, and the community was splitting apart. I made an immediate decision to leave on the next flight out because our safety was at risk. I had the week-end ahead of me to pack our necessary items. I took the school truck to get the boxes to the airport with the help of my vice-principal. Somehow I managed to keep my movements quiet until we showed up for the flight out to Saskatoon. The airport staff alerted the Chief who came to the airport just as we were about to board the plane. It was too late for him to change my mind. I was leaving in spite of his promises that it would work out well for both of us. I left the reserve formally taking stress leave. In truth, I was beyond stressed out.

We returned to our home in Elrose letting all know that I had finished my assignment at Fond du Lac. We then wasted no time in planning a quick vacation to Cancun, Mexico with a neighbouring couple, our best friends. The week in Mexico should have been a great vacation given perfect weather, but I found myself slipping into a depression. At times I would stay behind in our resort suite while my wife went out with our friends. In the privacy of our suite, I again found myself being nude. It took a few days before I could finally shake off enough of the depression to enjoy the days that remained. In the background, behind my smiles, I knew I had failed again, and blamed myself for the result.

At that point, we both agreed that I just wasn't cut out for the politics of education. The fact that we didn't need the money only made the decision to not apply to another school that much easier. In spite of that, I again was adrift. I still needed to do something to feel useful. I was too young to retire into a rocking chair. I remembered the idea of teaching at a university that I first talked about as a high school student in grade ten. It was a dream that couldn't happen without my returning to study for a doctorate, an option I wasn't ready to consider. So what did I want to do that I could do?

I began to search for the next best thing, teaching at a university in another country as an instructor. I set my hopes for China, a place that had been of interest since my teen years. I found several advertisements for university jobs in China and applied for one in a city called Changzhou, not too far from Shanghai. I sent an e-mail and received a quick response asking for my resume, photos and a copy of my passport. They replied the next day telling me that I had a job with them and that I needed to get a visa and sign the contract which they would e-mail to me. I asked about a job for my wife, telling them it was the only way I would take a job with them. She was given a position as a conversational English teacher. We were sent contracts for the next school year.

Chapter Seventeen

Our China adventure was just that, a real adventure. For the next two years we navigated through the customs and rituals of university academic life and as expats in China. We were treated as V.I.P.s and I thrived.

There were problems of course, normal problems that had nothing to do with my life falling apart or being haunted by the ghosts of my past. The problems mostly concerned issues of communication and of cultural adjustment. It helped that I had been a teacher and was good at teaching. None of the other foreigners hired by the university had been teachers so they based their teaching on how they had been taught in North America or Australia. It didn't take long for the university to offer me a greater level of respect. In their eyes I was a master teacher and I had a lot to teach even the Chinese instructors who taught English as a Second Language.

With this higher level of appreciation, my ego was stroked. "Finally," I thought, "people are getting to see the real me." It was the first time in my life that people around me saw me as I wanted to be seen and known. Interestingly, but not surprisingly, with that praise and respect I worked harder and with more creativity.

It didn't take us long to venture out of the city to visit more distant places trusting to my planning skills and intuition. Before the arrival of winter we had visited Beijing, Shanghai, and Suzhou, cities that had a long history with which I was familiar. By the end of the first term we had decided to spend the six-week term break in the sub-tropical south of China in order to stay warm. Changzhou City didn't have central heating and it was very damp and cold.

We went to stay in a condo in Sanya, a place that was China's version of Hawaii. It wasn't long before my clothes came off and I sat on the condo's balcony to absorb the rays of the sun. After an initial tension and resistance, my wife conceded to my unexplained need for nudity, wondering what it was about me being in a tropical place which ended up with me being nude. I couldn't answer the question though I knew that there had to be something deep within that compelled this behaviour.

The six weeks passed quickly and left us both feeling glad that we had this unique Chinese experience, especially when the condo's owner joined us for many of our forays into the Hainan Island culture. We returned to Changzhou rested and ready to begin our second term at the university.

The second term saw our performances as teachers improve with Chinese teachers sitting in our some of our classes to see how we taught. Our students had given us the highest ratings of any expat teachers, as well as most Chinese teachers. During this second term, our neighbours in Elrose who had spent time in Mexico with us the year before, came to visit us for two weeks during which time we got to share our classes, our experiences, and our Chinese friends with them. I continued riding the emotional high through the rest of the school term.

When the next national holiday came in May, we travelled, again on our own, to Xi'an to see the Terracotta Warriors and the famed walled inner city. By the end of June, we were both relieved and excited to go home to Canada for the summer after having signed a contract for the next school year with a significant pay raise. We both needed time to unwind, to slow down and get our bearings back home before our son's wedding.

A summer to unwind soon changed into a summer of constant movement as we tried to recapture the months of lost time with our children, grandchildren and extended family. By the time we needed to leave and return to China, I was again wound up tight. Without realising it, I had sacrificed too much needed alone time. I had continued to place others before me, excessively. There had been opportunities for me to take time-outs for solitude and silence, but I passed on them believing that to take that time was an act of selfishness. There would be a cost to pay, as one always pays a cost for not taking care of one's psychological needs. But, this was the furthest thing from my mind. I was in a rush to recapture the peak experiences of our first year in China.

The second year began where the first had left off. If the first year saw us treated like V.I.P.s, the second year told us that we had risen even higher in esteem. We had made the local newspapers on a number of occasions which led to all sorts of business opportunities and guest appearances for which we were paid exorbitant fees. We were celebrities.

We spent the autumn break taking a riverboat tour of the Three Gorges Dam which more than matched all of our expectations. The breadth of the country and its diversity began to teach both of us just how little we really knew of other countries beyond what mass media had taught us. What I thought I knew was often incorrect. What else did I take as truths that would be proven to be false?

The end of the first term arrived quickly. We chose to spend four weeks of our term break in India. We had decided that this would be our last year teaching in China and that it would be only sensible to visit India which was nearby rather than to risk never seeing that country. Our decision to make this our last year was based on missing too much of our grandchildren's lives by being a half-world away.

The reality of India shocked both of us. There was nothing we had heard or experienced which could have prepared us for the chaotic, churning reality of India. For the first time I experienced culture shock. New Delhi was an overwhelming nightmare. The nightmare continued into the next day as I looked out the hotel window at dawn to see people sitting on a massive garbage heap injecting drugs into their emaciated and grimy bodies. A few hours later that first morning we entered into a different India, the India I had learned about over the years, the India of history and culture. It was as if the country had a split personality that gave it a Doctor Jekyll and Mr. Hyde personality. We saw the best and worst of what it was to be human in India.

It was a relief when we flew to the southwest of India to spend the last twelve days of our break on the beaches of Goa. Again we found ourselves in a tropical paradise, at least on the edges of the Indian Ocean. The photos we took during these last days tell a beautiful story, but it wasn't the full story. Something was stirring again within me like a cancer threatening to return to life. But, a return to teaching silenced the stirring.

A month into the second term, I went to Shanghai to see an uncle, my mother's younger brother. It was a day where I took time to show him around the city which I had become quite familiar. Strangely, there was an undercurrent of tension between us that I didn't understand at the time. But it wasn't long after before I realised that he had reminded me of his father, the man who had sexually molested me. It was an unfair response to my uncle as he had never showed the least indication of being like his father in that manner.

Our first child and her family came to spend two weeks with us in China. As before when our neighbours had visited the spring before, they took part in our life in Changzhou with side excursions to Beijing and Xi'an before they left at the beginning of April.

With their departure, it was hard to get back into the routines of teaching and evaluation as the end of the term approached, especially as we had not signed a contract to come back to teach in Changzhou at the university. Our China adventure was coming to a close and I worried. Without China to keep my ego centred, what was I going to do?

As the term drew closer to the end, the pull of going home brought an end to the slight dip into depression that I had experienced. Excitement took its place. Three of our grandchildren and our second daughter, would be waiting for us at the airport in Saskatoon. It had been a long nine months since they had last seen us and they were excited.

Chapter Eighteen

Back home in Canada, life became another busy round of family and friends and activity through the summer. The energy levels surged and surged and surged as we were constantly surrounded by family for the first six weeks back home. When the house finally became quiet, I set to work repairing the back patio deck. I needed to keep busy to stay out of trouble. My wife got involved with a Women's Build project. We both found tasks to keep us busy.

In September we again began another round of visiting family over a two month period which included visiting my mother. It seemed that no sooner had one journey ended then it was time to head out in a different direction for another journey. It was as if we were both, unconsciously avoiding being alone at home. It didn't take much of an excuse to find someone else to visit. We decided to book a three-month winter stay in Mexico during one of our travel lulls back in Elrose.

By the time November 2008 arrived, we took another road trip to see my wife's brother who was experiencing the onset of Alzheimer's. And then, it was off again to visit another set of grandchildren, and then another set of grandchildren, then our son and his new wife before returning home. We finished the year with all of our grandchildren and their parents coming to our home to celebrate Christmas with us. Somewhere in the midst of all of that activity, I set up a blog site focused on Jungian psychology.

In January 2009, we flew off to spend three months in Yucatan, Mexico. Were we running? If so, what were we running away from? Or, was it simply a well-reasoned plan to enjoy sunshine and warm temperatures during the coldest part of a Canadian winter?

We arrived in Chuburna, Yucatan, Mexico and were pleased with what we saw of our winter home at the southern edge of the Gulf of Mexico. It was a world away from the bustle of Cancun where we had stayed for a week only three years earlier. We were slow to begin our explorations beyond the paths we could walk for the first several weeks. We soon found ourselves immersed in an interpersonal quietness that had wind and waves as background noise. It was the first time for both of us in being left alone without the distraction of others and activities. And, for the most part, it was good.

However, it wasn't just being alone together and wondering what to do, what to say to each other to fill the long hours; we were faced with ourselves as individuals. We were both out of our natural elements of career, family, friends and community. There was just the two of us. Even life in China had somehow managed to fill most of our time with work, students, friends, and curious Chinese people. There was always something to do, someplace to go when the silence became too much. So, we did what we always had done in the past, we went exploring with the camera while walking for hours in every direction.

There was a difference this time while I wandered with the camera. The difference focused on a change in the filters used by my unconscious in selecting subjects and their presentation. In looking back, there is a noted focus on things broken and abandoned and in the feminine, the power of the feminine. One photo I took of my wife had her walking through a set of poles set into the water with her hands uplifted while a flock of seagulls appeared to be obeying her command to fly from their roosts on the posts. Somehow I had captured the image of a goddess, a magical image.

Ten days after arriving, we had come across the ruins of an old stone building only steps away from the seas. An old, dead skeleton of a tree stood between the ruins and the beach. As had begun to be my practice, I took photos and wrote a blog post to go with the photo. The post exposed more than information of the scene, it set the opening scene for a journey of my self-exploration that would continue for years into the future, a journey that is still in progress as I write this book:

> "The roots of the tree are found at the beach's edge, where the brush meets the sand, only metres away from the seashore. Like the ruins which are out of view, the tree is stripped bare, exposed to the core. I identify with this tree and somehow that is a bit troublesome. What if I were stripped bare of all the masks, all the ruses and illusions

created by my conscious and unconscious self?" [January 15, 2009]

I had found myself resisting what was appearing on my life path, I focused as much as possible on staying undercover, preventing my inner self from being exposed and vulnerable. It became a battle of control, self-control. Who would win the battle, my soul or my ego? I had worked too hard in the past to achieve some sort of psychological wellness. That work was done and there was no way that I was going to go back down that road again.

> *"As for my inner self, I know I don't hardly try enough to take care of psyche as I do of my physical home. And in noticing the simplicity of a Mayan home, I realised that the undressed 'self' has its own beauty, a natural beauty."* [January 30, 2009]

There was a woman living alone in the casa beside ours, a woman who became friends with us, a friend for my wife for the rough months that lay ahead of us as a couple. I had begun a psychological journey that had been delayed for too long. We also had friends from our home in Canada staying in the nearby town of Progresso for the winter, friends who joined forces with us on a road trip through the Mayan Yucatan and the mangrove swamplands near Rio Lagartos. As always, I took a lot of photos of birds, architecture, people, and other curious things that caught my eye. In spite of the novelty and my natural curiosity about this country which was so different in so many ways from my own, I had slipped into a quietness that signalled an approaching depression.

Back at our casa, a place that had become our home of sorts, we frequently found ourselves retreating into the house in the evening to escape the strong, cold winds coming off the water, winds that forced us to close the shutters to keep out the salt spray. I retreated quietly into myself and became increasingly self-critical. I was unworthy of this woman. I knew that buried somewhere deep within me was a darkness that would challenge both of us in the years ahead. And, I doubted that what we had together would hold when that darkness emerged. So, I fought the darkness back, forcing it back behind my forced smiles and a determination to focus more on being present. And, I continued to write.

> *"I also sense that the tree is an inner self that refuses to be contained by the artificial walls that we build to protect our sense of self, an insecure self that will beg others for positive affirmation. Try as hard as one wants, cracks will appear in the façade, our insecurities will slip out as unconscious contents so that we aren't even aware of the cracks. In the end, we wonder, "What the hell has just happened?"* [February 5, 2009]

As February passed in a flurry of activity with Mardi Gras in Merida, and a road trip to Uxmal with our neighbour and one of her American friends; we ventured off the beaten trails of Chuburna to wander at the edges of the local mangrove swamps. Walking along the edges of the swamp, it was as though I found myself in a too familiar place, an odorous place that held dangers unseen beneath the surface of the water.

At times, I would wander off alone with my camera. On sunny days I would stop behind an old abandoned building near the sea and sit in the shelter of a wall, facing the sun. I simply wanted to soak in the heat of the sun, to feel myself being cooked. Then, on one such day, ensuring I was hidden by a dune on one side and the wall on the other so that passing beach walkers couldn't see me, I stripped of my clothing, and bared my body to the sun. For those few minutes, I was totally vulnerable. Under the intense rays of sunshine, the darkness I felt at the edges of my mind, disappeared allowing me to breath.

It was the beginning of a new chapter in my life, a very difficult chapter that would test my sanity and my relationship. I was turning to nudity, unconsciously as I had turned to nudity when I had been a teenager, in an attempt to stay sane and cope with what I could only call the hungry ghosts of my past.

Chapter Nineteen

The mangrove swamplands pulled at me. I was getting more and more depressed as the weeks passed, and it seemed that the only moments of some sort of peace within myself, was when I found myself alone in the swamplands near our casa, or when I was nude in the sunshine. I knew that psychologically I was on the edges of a place of darkness, and that I had to make a journey through that darkness. I found myself thinking back to my Jungian studies and the words of Carl Gustav Jung to explain to myself what was going on:

> *"One does not become enlightened by imagining figures of light, but by making the darkness conscious.... For our own sake we have to explore the darkness or we cannot proceed with our lives. The task of midlife is not to look into the light, but to bring light into the darkness."*[9]

Back at the casa, I had stretched the tension of our relationship as I began to find other ways to be nude in the casa, and outside beside the casa where I thought I could still be in the sunshine and yet be protected from the eyes of others. My nudity became a source of conflict between us. Yet, it seemed the more I tried to keep my clothing on to avoid these conflicts, the more agitated I became only to enter into conflicts within myself. My depression challenged my will to stay within the boundaries that were needed by my wife.

Not wanting to risk my marriage, I began to take my nudity away from the casa into the swamplands. I would be alone out there walking in shallow water. My intuition and gut told me that I had work to do there in the swampland, a task that could no longer be postponed. I didn't have a family to raise anymore, or a career that I had to attend to anymore.

> *". . . there is no sunlit meadow, no restful bower of easy sleep; there are rather swamplands of soul where nature, our nature, intends that we live a good part of the journey, and from whence many of the most meaningful moments of our lives will derive. It is in the swamplands where soul is*

---

[9] Jung, A Modern Man In Search of Soul. p.

fashioned and forged, where we encounter not only the gravitas of life, but its purpose, its dignity and its deepest meaning."[10]

As I wandered through the swamplands, naked, or when I hid behind the dunes unclothed, I had opened a Pandora's Box within me, setting in motion a long, twisting journey of soul recovery.

But, it wasn't all darkness in Chuburna. There were many good days that appeared with the sunshine. The problem was that the mere existence of the dark days worried both of us who had lived through very dark times in the nineties when I had ended up in Calgary for analysis. I was sixty years old and retired. Midlife with its crisis had long passed. These years were supposed to be our golden years, not a return to darkness.

Darkness. There was something about darkness and light that acted as magnets to pull me into depths. The virtual depths of my psyche found a resonance in the depths of two sets of caves we entered near the end of our stay in Mexico. The Calcehtok Caves were discovered, as we drove a rented car through the Yucatan, in a non-descript field. There was a deep hole in which I could see trees and plants growing far below. A thin and fragile looking ladder was the only way down. A Mayan guide soon appeared and we descended into the large and deep opening. Once at the bottom, we began another more gradual descent into the bowels of the earth. Over the next few hours we moved from light into darkness. Every once in a while a hole in the rock above our heads would appear through which shafts of light would illuminate another area of life. This was the landscape of my dreams. I knew this place and I felt at home.

As the end of our stay in Mexico approached, I took another photo that haunted me, a picture that found its way onto the cover of the second book in this series, an image of a broken road through the swampland. The work I had begun, resisting it as much as I could but giving in hoping to save my sanity, was what I could best describe as alchemical. Think of how elements are broken down to their basic components then put into a forge to create a stronger

---

[10] Hollis, James, Swamplands of the Soul: Finding Life in Dismal Places, p.

object. I was being broken down, cooked under the heat of the sun and in the process, changing. I managed to capture that feeling in one of my March, 2009 blog posts that featured the same photo:

> "*The alchemical work that is in progress while I am here in Mexico is being flooded with so many images that it makes sense to me that it is all about change. I don't know yet if that is good or bad in terms of where I have been and where I am going. . . . the transformation is not necessarily going to be gentle. The journey looks to be rough and solitary. It can't be any other way. So I wait and wonder . . .*" [March 25, 2009]

Near the end of our time in Chuburna, I found a new project that breathed life back into me, brought me relief from the pressing shadows. There was a SoFoBoMo challenge that I learned about, the challenge to produce a photo book within a thirty day time period. I immediately began to go through my photos to get an idea of what I would do for that challenge. Seeing a photo of some flamingos that I had taken which was a poor photo in comparison to the others because I had not extended my telephoto extender lens far enough, I had created a photo in a tunnel effect.

My first impression was to see if I could use that technique on purpose to create a set of round photos with a black background focused on the swampland that had become my personal space. For the next two weeks I took photos and wrote about the swamplands and depression based on the poem, Dark Soul of the Night, by Saint John of the Cross. I published the little book on the web and felt confident enough to enter my name into the challenge which was set for late spring. The book challenge had given me a sense of purpose. I began to see that whatever lay ahead of me on the path I was following, writing and publishing was going to be a significant part of that journey.

On the fifth of April, we returned to our home on the prairies.

Chapter Twenty

We arrived at home a few days before Easter, and soon had our two oldest grandsons arrive with their parents. Life slipped back into normal routines of family, friends and community. There was one addition, the photography book project with the objective of completing a photography book in thirty days. I continued to use the strategy for photos which appeared to be seen through a darkened tunnel which I had used for the swamplands booklet. I called the book, Tunnel Vision. I raced through the project only to challenge myself to completing a second full book, Discovering the Hero Within, during the same time frame. This was the beginning of the Though a Jungian Lens series of books. Again, I turn to my blog posts to try and understand what I was thinking that lead to that first book.

> *"Tunnel vision is part of my life, part of my journey. Thinking more about tunnel vision, I realised that we are all wandering through this earth dimension with tunnel vision, limited by our shadow, limited by how little of the personal and collective unconscious that we have yet faced. Tunnel vision limits not only our sense of 'self' but also our knowledge of 'other'.'* [April 11, 2009]

I noticed that already I have created a distance for myself. In giving the appearance that I am doing the work of healing, I shifted to a more philosophical position, one that sets me off to the side, out of the circle of my own attention. Hearing this in my words written on my return home from Mexico, I am reminded of that circle activity when I attended burnout camp for teachers while living in Lanigan. Contrary to outer appearances, I was again engaged in a disappearing act. My focus had turned to the outer world and the people in my life, doing my best to wear a smile and be the man they needed and loved. The last thing I wanted to happen was to again sink into another depression.

By the time summer arrived, both books had been completed, travels to visit grandchildren and time do some basement renovations, and the playing of numerous games of golf had left me exhausted. It was in this state of fatigue that was more psychological than physical when we returned to visit my brother-in-law who showed increasing signs of distress as the descent into Alzheimer's began to steal more and more of his memories and capacities.

A return home following this visit had me rethink my relationship with my own children, I had been writing quite a bit about father-complexes and masculinity over the preceding months and the idea of how the sins of the father get visited upon the children. With a gathering of all five of our grandchildren, all grandsons and our three adult children and their spouses, I had a lot to think about in terms of how my wounding in childhood had in turn wounded those that followed me.

> *"I wonder if the sins of the maternal grandfather get visited upon their grandsons. Somehow, I think they do in a curious way, through his daughter to her son. . . . I will dare to begin writing the story of my father, his father, and myself. This will be a gift to my son as well as my daughters and to my grandchildren."* [July 4, 2009]

Where had this resolve come from? Likely, it sprung from a need that had been left unmet. I had had issues with men in my life, my father, my maternal grandfather, and an assortment of adult males who had been authority figures in my life such as priests and administrators in schools and other places of employment. For whatever reason, that good intention to write this story was abandoned for several years. There had been a tiny glimpse of a bigger problem that would emerge two years later, the role of my mother in my wounding as a child. I got busy re-writing the story of a different man, my father-in-law. There was more safety in telling his story as he had told it to me, trying to fill in the blank spaces with research of the place and time of his youth in the Ukraine. I banished my story into forgetfulness, abandoned that story.

Life continued to be busy with us travelling to see our grandchildren and them returning to our house, as well as a never-ending series of golfing. Writing was kept simple as though not to disturb a gentle quietness within myself. Life was full, I was fully engaged in my outer life. Then following my sixtieth birthday, some inner disquiet began to be stirred, a feeling that I captured in one of my blog posts which began with a quotation:

> *"While we might on some days prefer to simply be happy carrots, relieved of our urgencies, our anxieties and impossible desires, we also suffer greatly when we are not living the life which the psyche wishes us to live. Such existential bad faith will always demand some payment – in the body, in our relationships, in our disturbing dreams, or in the burden our children will have to carry for us."* [11]

> *"Like most people, I beat back the urges, the voices, and dreams. Like others, I then have to pay the price in terms of my body. Sleep becomes more difficult and the dreams seem to taking on a louder voice in an attempt to have me recognize them. I don't want to go there. Instead of recording the dreams and thinking about them. The disquietude within is simmering. I don't want to go there. Why can't I be a happy carrot?"* [July 26, 2009]

Again we found ourselves on the road to and from family, including a special trip to celebrate the birth of our sixth grandson. I was very aware that with this grandson, the line through fifteen generations of my paternal heritage signalled that the family line would continue on through this little baby boy.

We then made plans in the late summer to head south to Costa Rica for the winter before heading out the door of our home once more for an extended visit to British Columbia which would take us in and out of many extended family homes before returning to our own home in time to prepare for Christmas with all of our children and grandchildren before we boarded a plane to another tropical country.

---

[11] Hollis, James, On This Journey We Call Our Life, p. 12

Chapter Twenty-One

The rush to discover the treasures of Costa Rica was in stark contrast to the gradual explorations we had experienced in the Yucatan, Mexico. My camera was kept busy providing me with all sorts of interesting images. Even when we settled into our condo in Playa Jaco, we spent a lot of time exploring. It took almost two weeks before we began to finally relax and establish new patterns for our life in Coast Rica.

The Pacific Ocean had captured our attention as we headed out almost every evening to watch the sunset, almost hypnotised by the colours of Costa Rican sunsets. It was at this time, two weeks in this paradise, that I sensed a return of disquietude, or dis-ease. The heat of the sun had begun to affect me as if I had been a pot of water left on a stove burner, simmering before bursting into a bubbling out of inner stuff that had been held onto for too long. Not aware of the darkness beginning to seep out, I was caught by surprise resulting in another conflict with my wife. She had been down this road before and was becoming more and more anxious about my mental health, and angry with me for turning paradise into Hell.

> *"I was feeling conflicted and low in a way, but not really depressed, just a bit lost and empty. Life does that to a person. I sometimes get so into my head, so into the sky, that I lose sight of what lies beneath the sky. And, in being lost in the sky, I fail to notice that I have begun to operate unconsciously, not my usual somewhat aware self. And in doing so, conflict finds its way back into the picture as I rail against this incursion of shadow into my "self." I can't wander unconsciously acting in ways that spill out either, something that happens when I get too caught up in my head."* [January 13, 2010]

As the conflicts began to mark our relationship, I once again took to stripping off my clothing. In behind our studio was a tiny walled space just big enough for me to use as a private sunbathing area. It wasn't long before I needed this private time. I found myself agitated when I couldn't get that private, healing time. And, the agitation of denied nudity found its way into my dreams. Or, likely it was the agitation of my dreams, the stirring of repressed inner contents that found its way into my behaviours and attitudes in my waking life, and into our relationship.

I recorded one dream that spoke to the issue of my masculinity:

> *". . . I am in a conflict with a woman I don't know and feel a sense of impending loss . . . I turn to her and ask her why she is leaving me, why she is abandoning me . .. she tells me it is because I have a penis . . . the conflict continues and the stakes seem to be rising . . . I again ask her why she is leaving me . . . she tells me that my penis is not huge and hard enough . . ."*

What had happened? I knew enough about dreams to know that this wasn't about my wife and myself, and that it had to be something else. I knew that the appearance of a female in a man's dream has to do with either the anima, that is the feminine nature of a man that is best known as his soul; or, there has been an archetype activated, that of the Mother. What was the message coded into my dream? Was I finding myself lacking as a man, perhaps feeling emasculated because of ongoing conflicts with my wife? The dream doesn't give answers, it simply lets my psyche know it was time to pay careful attention. Sexuality, sexual identity, body awareness: so much was rising up from the depths, contaminating and challenging our marriage.

My nudity was becoming more and more of an issue between us as I fought to gain control of what was happening to me. I struggled with myself, angry with myself. Why was I nude? It was in the middle of this struggle that saw me take the nudity out from the private enclosure into the condo itself. I took my nudity into our shared space. My nudity became like a poison as it crept into her space, her only place of normality in our tiny condo. I retreated and tried harder to keep my clothing on when she was in the condo, making sure that I used only the tiny, tiny sunspace at the back of the condo. My efforts failed as they always seemed to fail. What kind of a husband was I not to give my wife what she needed from me? She wasn't denying me the right to be nude; she only asked that there was a need for boundaries for her own well-being.

Near the end of our first month in Jaco, I took a photo of myself which I then photoshopped into a photo of a full moon. I called the photo *the man in the moon* and placed it on my blog site. It was the second nude photo of me that had ever been taken. The first had been taken by my wife while we were in Cuba in December 2004. In the post with the photo, *the man in the moon*, I wrote:

> "*Being transparent, allowing the unconscious contents to inform consciousness so that we have the courage to cease being desperately straight-jacketed . . . The image of the Vitruvian Man is all about wholeness ... the presentation of the Vitruvian Man as a nude by Leonardo da Vinci, is all about transparency, about stripping away of masks and being able to see the true man, vulnerable and yet powerful for all vulnerability.*" [January 29, 2010]

I was stunned and very uncomfortable with what was happening to me, surprised that it had spilled into the public space of my Jungian blog site. I was afraid more than anything else, afraid that I was putting our marriage in jeopardy. All that was going through my head, was about my relationship and how I was messing it all up. I didn't know what to say to try and fix what I felt was becoming broken, broken because of my actions, my dysfunctional behaviours. Ashamed, I retreated into silence and tried over and over again to banish the practice of nudity. I was resisting being nude as hard as I could, and all it was doing was making my problems worse.

Because I had basically kept my nudity within the tiny enclosure, my wife was accepting this nudity within boundaries better than I was. She saw the difference in me when I was risking sunbathing and when I resisted sunbathing. I began to trust a bit more in the process as she spoke positively about my needs as long as I kept that nudity in its proper place. She gave me permission to be nude. I greedily took this permission and relaxed while in the enclosure, without worrying about her anger. I had her permission. I hadn't yet learned that I needed to give myself permission. A mother-complex had intruded into my relationship more visibly than it had done so in the past.

Relaxing, I continued to read and to write. It helped me as I gained a bit more of my self-authority as I read the words written by Daryl Sharp, a Jungian analyst and author, who encouraged the reader, in this case, me, to work on myself in order to work on my relationship

> *"Work on yourself and a good relationship will follow. You can either accept who you are and find a relationship that fits, or twist yourself out of shape and get what you deserve."*[12]

Therein lay the problem. Would the relationship that fitted me be the relationship with my wife? I had to trust in her to still want me in her life as I did the work on myself that was demanding my attention. But, I didn't trust myself enough and couldn't see how she could accept the stranger that I was becoming. Could I, would I follow the good advice from Sharp?

Daring to enter in this work on myself took me into a study of psychological alchemy, a study of how one changes or transforms into a more authentic person. I began to understand the pull I experienced towards being nude, the unconscious motive to my being cooked by the sun. And that awareness, lead to take a second nude photo of myself. The photo was edited for colour saturation to match the four stages of alchemical psychological transformation. I entered into the study of alchemy as a novice. As I moved through the process, as I understood it, who I was would be transformed over and over again one bit at a time. And, in the process my changed self would result in others around me changing to respond to my transformations.

As I moved through the days of intense sun with no rain in sight, I again found myself questioning myself. What the hell was the matter with me? Why was I not as happy as I should be? I had everything that I needed and wanted. I had financial security. I had the freedom of movement and speech and I had a good home in a safe country. I had healthy and financially secure children with their own homes and young families. I had it all. Yet, I didn't feel as though I had anything. I didn't have any respect for myself. I didn't understand who I was or what was happening to me.

---

[12] Sharp, Daryl, Jung Uncorked: Book 2, p. 23

A final image of me nude found its way onto my blog site at the end of March, less than a week before our departure to return home to Canada. It was an attempt to depict Rodin's *The Thinker*, one of the ways that I see myself in this world. I was desperately trying to find some sense of identity, of being somewhat normal rather than a throw-away man.

We returned home and life again returned to *normal* patterns. The time in Costa Rica had been rich in so many ways; it hadn't just been about my inner turmoil. Together we had explored volcanoes, rain forests, Mayan sites, and mountain sides filled with exotic birds and animals. In spite of the beauty, though, those months in Costa Rica were tarnished with regret, anger, and my depressive episodes.

And as with other years, I was soon overwhelmed with my seasonal allergies and life in general. The loss of a retreat place to bathe in the rays of the sun, mixed in with the return of my allergies, deepened my depression. Discouraged, I almost considered abandoning the work transformation through self-healing. Thankfully, I finally was beginning to understand myself and why I needed to retreat, rather than abandon the process.

> *"I think of how I retreat for short periods of time behind a layer or mask in community, take on a layer that looks like one I used to wear so that those around me can then recognise me. The layer is temporary. Sometimes I retreat into a revised layer in order to give myself a rest from the journey.*
>
> *Going from retirement back into teaching at a university in China is a good example of this. I retreat into an older persona and invest energy and time and avoid the journey as if it was the plague. Yet, beneath that revised layer, I know the truth and can't still the voices I am coming to recognise only too well. As a result, the persona shifts to accommodate a more conscious self-awareness. I am now a different kind of teacher as I re-emerge.*

The journey is cyclical, I retreat into dormancy like a plant into winter, only to re-emerge in the spring with a newer version of myself – one that will also retreat into dormancy and then re-emerge. This isn't a new idea. The changes aren't always positive, sometimes they are regressive. Sometimes I choose to not do the work of enlarging my narrow slice of consciousness and retreat into darkness and shadows as if still a victim." [April 26, 2010]

It didn't take long before the rounds of visiting family, the return to the golf course with men who had become my community friends, and the tasks of maintaining my home filled the hours and days. Whatever it was that I had thought I had discovered about myself retreated. It was as if I had entered a winter season, a time of no psychological growth while waiting for spring and my rebirth as a changed man.

Waiting in the background, worried about my lassitude and lethargy, my wife struggled as well not knowing how to support me while at the same time wondering when the ordeal would finally end. It seemed as though conflicts had left both of us blaming ourselves for triggering the night storms that left us drained for days. When the storms passed, we would turn to each other, holding each other knowing that life without each other was a thought too unbearable to entertain. Yet, for me, the threat of being abandoned, of being tossed out as not worth the effort to continue our marriage was my greatest fear.

"I wonder at times about being alone, sometimes thinking that it would be easier, that there would be fewer distractions, fewer interruptions. What books I might then write, what photos I might then take, what learning about "self" I might then discover! But each time I find myself alone, I slip into lethargy and do less. Anxieties seem to surface and paralyze.

I "know" that I must learn to bear the anxiety, but I cling to the hope that in relationship to an "other" I will be saved the pain of loneliness, that in relationship to an "other" I will have meaning and purpose." [May 27, 2010]

Relationships. I found myself writing constantly about relationships in my blog posts. Most of the blog posts focused on my relationship to the feminine, not my relationship to my wife. I was aware, psychologically, that this inner "feminine" was more about my relationship with my unconscious, my soul which I had abandoned and projected onto others beginning with my mother.

I worried about losing my wife as I became more aware of my defects. In my psychological centre, it was I who had abandoned my own soul, selling my soul to the devil, so to speak, while a child in order to stay sane enough to do all that was expected and needed of me. And, as a man, as a husband, as a father, and as a school leader I had held onto that early life script.

I had frequently been told that I became like a child during our conflicts leaving her to feel like the "bad, controlling mother." I hadn't yet made the connection between my triggered responses and the deep underlying causes of a mother-complex that needed to be addressed. It was the mother-complex and not the father-complex that was now demanding my attention. And, I resisted like some defiant child disobeying his mother. And, as often had happened in the past, what I was reading in Jungian psychology books echoed what was happening in my outer life.

I had turned once again, to a book I had read more than a decade earlier, by James Hollis as part of my plans for yet another photo book that would become the fourth book in the Through a Jungian Lens series. And as always when I returned to an old book, ideas I had missed in earlier readings leap out to capture my attention as they spoke to the undercurrents that had not quite made it into my consciousness, my rational awareness.

> "So a man, during the Middle Passage, has to become a child again, face the fear that power masks, and ask the old questions anew. They are simple questions: "What do I want? What do I feel? What must I do to feel right with myself?" Few modern men allow themselves the luxury of such questions. So they trudge off to work and dream of retiring to play golf on some Elysian Field, hopefully before

the heart attack arrives. Unless he can humbly ask these simple questions and allow his heart to speak, he has no chance whatsoever. He is bad company for himself and others."[13]

Those same questions had been asked of me during our night storms. Typically, I retreated into childlike responses, triggered knee-jerk responses that should have informed me that I was under the spell of a complex, my mother-complex. Because I was in the grips of a complex, there was no rational way I could hear and respond to those basic questions that kept being repeated and repeated each time the night storms raged around us.

It was less than a week after posting this same quotation on my blog post that I found myself on a plane headed to visit my mother. I was going to be the first time I would have gone to see her alone since I had met my wife forty years earlier. As I flew to visit my mother and her consort, I had hopes of talking with her about my father. I had hoped to get answers that would fill in the gaps of my memories. The real purpose of my visit was to deal with her worsening health issues that were making her independent living increasingly difficult to maintain. And, as always when I visited, I stayed at her home.

While visiting her, I found the need to escape too often, looking for excuses to walk through the town or to drive to another town using my brother's truck. I knew I "should" be spending the hours with her and the guilt weighed heavily. Yet, I had to escape. I soon became a regular visitor at a coffee house where I could hook into the Internet and write my blog posts.

While in my mother's community, I took photos for my next book for the photography book series, Sol and Luna – the Sun and the Moon. I was unable to get any "moon" photos while there. The moon was evasive, as evasive as my mother who refused to talk about anything from my years growing up as her first born child. All that she would tell me, and anyone else in hearing distance, was that I was the perfect son, her "golden child."

---

13 Hollis, James, The Middle Passage, p. 55

By the time I left her place, arrangements had been put into place to enable her to move into assisted-living accommodation. It was left to my brother who lived nearby to help make it happen. My job had been to get her to finally agree to our plans for her care. I returned home and completed the book, Sol and Luna, the fourth in the series, Through a Jungian Lens.

Back home, the decision was made to return to teach at the same university in China. We both realised that I needed to be teaching, to have that purpose in my life for my mental health. The university in Changzhou willingly accepted our application to return. Since there wasn't a lot of time to go through the process of obtaining visas and preparing for the return to China, I made a quick trip to Calgary where I could get the proper visas within a day.

While in the city, I visited with the male Jungian analyst, ZM, whom I had almost chosen to be my analyst twelve years earlier. We had been communicating via e-mail about Jungian topics, something I had also been doing with another Jungian analyst and author from Ottawa. I had thought our meeting was to be about discussing the ideas that I had written about in my book. ZM had a different understanding of the purpose of my visit, likely because of what my body language was telling him. It became more of an analysis session that a discussion. He focused on father-complex that was still eating at me, especially since my recent visit to my mother's place. I got angry and left. ZM had struck a vital nerve and I needed to escape rather than confront that throbbing wound.

The frustration with my mother soon made itself felt in my dreams, which then reappeared in my choices of reading materials to serve as blog posting themes. I had been focused on issues of the masculine in my life and in the life of outer world of power. There was a shift to recognise the feminine, and as always, that shift appeared first in a dream:

> "... I am with a woman, my partner ... it seems as if we are going golfing only I don't have my clubs with me ... I turn back to go and get them and I am met by two men ... I can tell they have evil in mind as they hold me ... I see a woman appear ... she doesn't have a natural colour, as though she is

injured, damaged ... I realist that she is dis-spirited as though she had no libido ... she is laying on the ground beside the road without clothing, a blue ghost of a woman ... from the left side, a young female child approaches her on hands and knees ... she looks at the blue woman as though talking to her but no words are spoken or heard ... I knew the child was asking for the blue woman to open her legs and expose her vulva ... the girl-child crawls to her and begins to place a kiss on the blue woman's nether lips ... and then I feel the men's grips tightening, holding me down so that the blue woman can rape me ... I know I have been raped, but not by the blue woman ... I am broken, as dispirited as the blue woman. ...” [July 12, 2010]

The images that became charged for me were all about my wife as a blue goddess, as a Magical Other. I had thought, at that time, that it was simply a shift for my blog site. However, it was really a shift that was about something very personal, very powerful in me. It wasn't about the archetypal mother, about Mother Earth. It was about my mother and my mother-complex.

I wasn't yet aware of any personal mother issues and began to think that it was simply more about my guilt for not being the “golden son,” she had bragged about. The visit to my mother had left me incredibly frustrated. I had hoped to fill in the holes only to be met with dismissive denials. Whatever was festering below the surface was rising up in my dreams and then spilling over into my blog posts.

I was glad when the decision to leave home again was made and formalized. All that was left was to make the rounds of visiting, attend weddings family reunions and golf. Together, in the last days before we began the journey that would take us back to Changzhou, we prepared our house for our ten-month absence.

Chapter Twenty-Two

We flew to Toronto. We had planned on several days with our son and his young family in Toronto where he had relocated for his career. It was our turn to say goodbye to them before disappearing for ten months. Then, we flew off to the Far East. It is strange as I look back in time to this returning to China that my first post to my blog site when back in China was called *"Anima Activated."* The feminine within was reawakening and was being paired with the feminine essence of my wife.

Though I thought I was conscious of who I was and what I wanted, my written words told a different story. It was as if I had become wilfully blind, hiding behind my own masks and camouflage. I thought I knew myself well enough to discuss my "self" in psychological terms as I wandered through Jungian ideas on the blog site. The truth was, I was hiding in an attempt to deny the darkness, using the foreignness of China as a backdrop with which I could deceive myself.

In my blog entry for September 1, 2010, I wrote:

> *"I lack the courage and the temperament to stick out, to risk being in full view of others. I prefer to keep low and stick to the shadows and not be noticed all that much, at least most of the time. Personally, I prefer to take risks and go out on a limb within my inner landscapes. There I know I have my privacy, safety, and there I have the courage to do what I would never consider doing in the outer world. So, what does that say about me?"*

The evidence left behind me over the years in the wake of dealing with my psychological issues, left behind in full public view, tell a different story. I had made my pain public in local newspapers, in books, in private conversations, in the world of cyberspace conversations, and in my numerous blog posts, including three written earlier the same year that contained nude images of me. I was creating a fraudulent image of myself for myself. I was hiding, running away from some very vital truths about myself that needed to be freed from the prisons built in decades long past, built before I knew the woman I would marry. Here I was at the age of sixty-one, standing out like some famous V.I.P. in a foreign country, a different race and culture. Here I was, the Master Teacher reveling in that role, a very public role in a city of four and a half million people where I was featured on the front page of newspapers on more than one occasion.

The city of Changzhou had changed as much as I had changed in the two years since we were last there. In spite of those changes, I charged into the world of teaching with confidence. My writing focused on being a teacher of depth psychology concepts. And in my role as lead teacher for the expats, I was given the role of mentoring, a role that resonated as I had once mentored teacher in my schools when there was a need. My ego swelled and again hubris blinded me to the small cracks that began to show up in the privacy of our apartment home. What was going on behind my conscious control? The answer was buried in one of my posts, *"with a complex activated, the drama unfolds and life becomes a confused mess."*

In spite of the changes, the initial energy in being back in an environment that saw my ego validated in so many ways, made the first months of teaching race by. However, like a person suffering from bipolar disease, that initial "high" wore thin and the "lows" were waiting patiently in the wings.

In October 2010, we were given free passes into the World Expo being held in Shanghai. We both took the crowds in stride taking in as much of the Expo as possible before heading "home" to our apartment in Changzhou.

Back home, the signs of another period of depression began to appear. They showed up in small conflicts at home. My growing awareness of these moments of dis-ease seeped out into my blog posts:

> *"When a relationship hits a rocky patch, it pretty much looks like everything is going downhill, down into a dark hole. One's field of vision is reduced to a narrow band of possibility, and the possibility is in darkness, a damp darkness that reminds one of a swampland at night where*

sinkholes are just waiting to suck one down. In an instinctive reaction we lash out hoping to back off the demons and find a bit of breathing space. The enemy is out there, and the enemy is wearing the body of one's partner in relationship." [October 24, 2010]

Projections were again at work within me. Triggers were being activated. I had had thought I had deactivated the triggers to avoid having the dangerous inner demons to escape and trash my life. My wife became the victim of my fears responding to the shadows that danced and approached. Though I knew she wasn't the enemy, the activated complexes didn't care what I knew, they were determined to get out of their prisons and get their day to speak and to teach me lessons about who and what I was. And so, I began to build a wall between myself and my wife, trying to keep her safe from my demons. I didn't know what to tell her or how to tell her what couldn't be said with words.

The life of teaching continued with only a few minor bumps, before the end of the first term. We had chosen a four-week tour of Indochina for our free time with most of that time to be spent in Vietnam. The last few days before our departure erupted into an issue between myself and my cooperating teacher. For the first time in China, I felt a lack of trust and respect as a teacher. At least that was how I read it at the time. But in retrospect, it was really about a female wanting to control me. I resisted and made a lot of waves in the department. The foundation for continued conflict had been sown between the two of us with neither of us willing to back down. We both were concerned with saving face.

Thankfully, the diversion of Vietnam, Laos, and Cambodia did a lot to heal tension within me, as well as making the rest of the school year stress free until it was time for final evaluations of the students in June when again I found myself clashing with the cooperating teacher.

Chapter Twenty-Three

We flew into Ho Chi Minh City on January 13, 2011 and I began to experience yet another shift in culture. I had assumed from my preparations, that I would see Vietnam through a masculine filter, a land with a long history of war, a country that is filled with temples and other structures that celebrated the masculine. Yet my journal told a different story.

> "*Water – the unconscious – anima – my soul. Somehow, the feminine has stepped forward to claim my attention. I have taken almost two thousand photos in five days and I would have to say that images of women and water account for most of these images. I do find men in this collection of photos and the temples that men have built, but not all that many. I am often disconcerted as women look into my eyes and smile with invitation while I walk down the streets of the towns and cities while holding M's hand.*" [January 19, 2011]

The Buddhist temples and the symbols found in so many places, as we travelled through Vietnam, awoke a desire within me to return to the practice of meditation. In the past I had used meditation as a means to find my own centre, a practice that would help quieten the shadows and ghosts hidden within me. But, I pushed the idea of meditation back, telling myself that it wasn't yet time, that I had too few hours in Indochina for meditation.

Two weeks after our arrival in Vietnam, we boarded a plane in Hanoi to fly to Laos, a country that felt like the holiest country I have ever been in, at least that is the way it felt to me. The face of Buddha was found in almost every aspect of the country. That sense of holiness that I had projected out there was only a reflection of what was happening within me. I was being pulled into a spiritual place of awe and wonder. Not only darkness lay within me, there was a matching sense of holiness, a pinpoint of golden light for me to follow out of that inner darkness.

I took a photo in Luang Prabang of a young man casting out a net from the shoreline into the Mekong River and wrote in my journal:

"I feel somewhat like this young man, casting my net out into the waters of the unconscious in hopes of netting something that will feed me, and perhaps feed others. So I continue this journey of images through Indochina. The images will bring ripples to my psyche and result in moving further down a road I know I am supposed to be travelling." [January 30, 2011]

There were many ripples that resonated from the images which numbered into the thousands in spite of my constantly deleting images each day. I sensed that it would be in the images that I would perhaps later find what I missed with my senses, knowledge that was buried deep within my unconscious. The images weren't just about recording our trip, they were more than that. They were evoking hidden truths.

As we travelled, we met with so many faces of poverty that we both felt our hearts break, especially when the faces of poverty were of children. The children were dirty, usually naked and vulnerable to whatever brutality that chose them as victims. Seeing them, I saw my own naked vulnerability as a child, relived the senseless poverty, the disconnectedness, the feeling of being lost. Yet, in spite of that poverty, the nakedness, and the dirt, the children we met were still able to play while surrounded by garbage. I felt guilty for having so much as an adult while these children had as close to nothing as it was possible to get.

From Laos we travelled into Cambodia to experience the wonders of Angkor Wat, Angkor Thom, and Bayon. The ruins left us speechless and filled with awe. And then, we travelled through floating cities. Always, there was the presence of a past that had been so brutal to humans, a past of despots and privileged royalty which impoverished the country.

While in Cambodia, in the city of Phnom Penh I took a photo of a baby sleeping in a dumpster that was filled with trash with a family seated next to the dumpster. I knew that they were street people. The image of the baby sleeping in the dumpster haunted me for days after arriving in Nha Trang, Vietnam. In Nha Trang I had time for thinking, for decompressing before heading back to Changzhou and the privileged life of a university instructor.

> *"The baby sleeping in the trash cart is symbolic of the self, a self that is denied as we buy into the persona we find ourselves in at birth and the personae we build more luxurious prisons in order to escape the prisons in which we were born. We come to believe we are the masks we wear, that the shadows we flee from are "others" and not really "our" own shadows. We disown and disinherit the baby in the trash cart. This is how we end up working so hard to drown the denied baby self in all manner of substances and activities. Yet, the baby reappears at night in our dreams, pleading for us to remember self, to reinvest in self. The baby is a symbol of promise and hope, letting us know that all is not lost, that we are not lost."* [February 9, 2011]

I was angry. I was angry at the world for allowing such poverty. I was angry with myself for being so quiet in the face of what was happening in the outer world that was seeing the wealthy become wealthier at the expense of babies and children. I felt shame that I had more than I needed yet powerless to change the situation. I knew that even if I gave everything I had to help the poor, the money would only go to feed the voracious hunger of the obscenely rich leaving me as destitute as the beggars I would have tried to help. I felt guilty for having escaped the poverty of my own childhood. I was angry. I needed to step back from it all and breathe, to let time and space dissipate the inner rage.

Chapter Twenty-Four

It was almost with relief that we returned to Changzhou. It wasn't yet time to return to classes, so we were both able to re-establish our bearings in our home in China. As I waited to return to the classroom, I had a lot of time for reflection. My lesson plans were all in place as were my term plans. I had brought back to Changzhou more than ten thousand photos and I had blogged frequently while in Indochina on my Jungian Lens site.

Why was I so taken with Jungian psychology and with photos? Why did I take those particular images? These were just some of the questions that arose while I sat in my apartment staying somewhat warm. For whatever reason that I had yet to discover, photography had become a very critical part of my psychological processing, my search for meaning and self-definition.

I turn again to my journal to illustrate the questions that pre-occupied me, and what I had then thought of as answers. The words presented in the journal also pointed to what was yet to come in terms of how I needed to continue my psychological journey to better self-awareness.

> *"It's no wonder that I resonate with so much of Jungian psychology. Images are vital to how I interact with the world. The images aren't only those found in my photos, they are also found in music, my words, in my dreams, and in the appearance that I present of myself to the world. Images are also found in the way I speak to others."* [February 17, 2011]

Images, numinous images that seem to be a portal to a different dimension, a fractal dimension exposing a universal rather than a personal truth. There was no question that the separation between inner and outer world was blurring for me. As well, I appeared to be connecting to a collective shadow that plunged me into a different kind of depression. Earthquakes, tsunamis, wars, politics, the voracious greed of bankers and corporations were eating at the soul of the world, and in turn, my soul. The time I had spent in Indochina had softened my core, made me more sensitive to the world around me. I sensed that it wasn't to be long before something broke loose within me. I just didn't know when that was going to happen.

And then spring came with sunshine and colours to lift my spirits. The emerging colours of spring banished the pressing shadows around me. Then, we had a visitor come to stay with us for a week from Canada. Life was easing back into normal with my energies returning so that I could teach with more passion again.

My writings on my blog sites continued to plumb psychological depths with my ego thinking that I was teaching others about Jungian psychology. But in truth, the selection of photos and the reflections that swirled around Jungian ideas had a different purpose which I had begun to realize. In my journal, on March 27, 2011, I wrote:

> *"I am discovering, uncovering my "self" in a way that is transparent and honest. There is nothing to hide, nor any reason to hide that which I discover, as the bits of shadow exposed enter into my consciousness and cease to be shadow."*

I had unconsciously begun a journey into more depth work. Time was running out for being normal. I was going to have to take some serious time outs to do the work being demanded by my psyche. But, that time was deliberately put on hold as we signed our contracts to work another year at the university. I wasn't ready to do the work at least that is what I told myself.

We finished giving our last exams early and returned to Canada the second week of June with a stop off in Toronto to visit our son and his family. No sooner had we landed, then my allergies reappeared. It seemed so strange how the allergies retreated into the background while we were in China, Mexico and Costa Rica, but when back in Canada, they reappeared with a vengeance.

I had made arrangements to have an appointment in Toronto with an allergy specialist in order to try a different approach to solving the problem of my allergies. It was the first step in what I could consider a re-making of myself in the world. I was tired of being a victim of my body. I loved my home in Canada and there just had to be some way to allow me to enjoy my Canadian home. The status quo just had to change. It was time.

Chapter Twenty-Five

One of the first things I did upon reaching our home on the Canadian prairies was to book our return flights to China. Because of the planned vacation of the allergy specialist in Toronto, I needed to return earlier than I had expected before we flew back to China. My wife decided she would fly later as she sensed that I needed some time alone without her. She knew that if she was present I would invest most of my energy in making the time in Toronto more about focusing on her than on myself.

With that business taken care of, we returned to our normal life at home with visiting, having visitors, golfing and enjoying the quiet of our house and yard when we were alone. That way of being *at home* was something that wasn't going to change. But, even at home there were changes happening, changes that stirred up new conflict. I had begun to be nude in our house. I began to meditate again sitting on cushions so that I could feel the cool air on my bared body, so that there were no body sensations that would distract me from the work of clearing my mind of racing and crazy thoughts.

The feeling of freedom, a freedom to breathe through my pores pulled me to explore even more about nudity. Those experiences showed up with a new focus on my blog site. I began to speak and write openly about nudity, naturism, sacredness, and authenticity. I was searching for truths about myself. Somehow the masks of ego and persona behind which I hid became reflected in how I felt I was also hiding behind my clothing. A remembered moment from the past when my middle child asked, *"Papa, what do you really look like?"* as she wondered about my face behind the beard I had worn for decades. Who was I beneath the beard? Who was I beneath the roles I lived? Who was I beneath the clothes I wore? Who was I beneath the skin?

My relationship with my body had been almost non-existent. In spite of the work, the running, the occasional skinny-dipping, my primary relationship with my *self* was with my *ego*, within my head. I had defined myself as philosopher and as a psychologist of sorts. I lived and thrived and suffered in my head. I didn't look in the mirror. Even photos of myself were rare. Somehow I had come to believe that Catholic dogma about the human body being the host of evil and darkness.

In contrast, nude meditation asked me to reconnect with my whole self. Two weeks after our return to Canada, I wrote my first blog post about naturism. That first post lead to three more including this entry in the second post:

> *"I know that I have found peace in nature, especially when clothing is set aside for a brief time. I have found that peace in lakes and in gentle pools along various rivers, walking through a Yucatan estuary, on protected areas along seashores, in isolated fields and meadows while walking down remote trails in the wilderness. This is not about social activity or about sexual gratification. This is about being honest with oneself, stripping away yet one more mask and exposing all the flaws so that they can be accepted as natural aspects of self rather than as deficits."* [June 25, 2011]

It wasn't long before I found myself going outside of my home, into abandoned places, empty spaces in the prairie hills in order to re-experience being skyclad, the stripping off of clothing outdoors in nature. My wife was accepting of my naturist activity as she had seen how nude meditation had been calming me at home. Her only concern was that I made sure that it was kept to places where no one would see me when I was nude outdoors. It was a promise I kept.

However, the addition of naturist posts to my blog site was a different story. Too many people we knew read the posts on my blog site. It was one thing to write about naturism in intellectual terms, but when it became personal, it was no different that stripping off my clothing in public. Whatever others saw about me and nudity impacted her. In response to my wife's concern, I created a new blog site devoted to naturism. Few people that we associated with knew of the naturist blog site. I didn't keep the site secret from my wife I made sure that I kept the blog site *safe,* with safe meaning no frontal full nudity with the full exposure of genitals. And, safe meant keeping the existence of the blog site quiet.

Walking in the hills away from farmhouses and our prairie town, I began to decompress significantly. As I walked the hills, I had my camera in my hand, as was very normal for me. I was able to take many photos of birds, deer, and the colours of the land and occasional appearance of water. I wandered skyclad. In nature I lost my old fear of being caught and exposed as a *dirty old man.* Less self-conscious I seemed to be able to get so much closer to the wildlife of the prairies. I was very aware of being naked, but not afraid of it. I was more curious than anything. It didn't take me long to wonder what would I see in images taken of myself while I was nude.

While exploring my identity beneath the camouflage of persona and clothing, I was also working on another book for the Through a Jungian Lens series, a book called Individuation. Many of the same scenes found in my naturist photos became part of the book. The book focused on nature alone, a face of nature always framed with a set of railway tracks serving as a symbolic thread of life from birth to death, from sunrise to sundown.

By the middle of July, 2011 we were fortunate to have all of our children and grandchildren gather at our home for a week. As always, their presence banished the shadows and showed me the positives in my life. I was a husband, father. Whatever self-meaning I had sought for in my psychoanalytical wanderings, a good portion of the meaning included being husband, father and grandfather.

A few days after they had gone, I made another trip to British Columbia to deal with ongoing issues with my mother and her health. She had begun to take dialysis treatments. She hadn't made the move into an assisted-living facility in her town, so my brother and I thought we could arrange for assisted living near the hospital where she had to get her treatments. We managed to convince her to have us appointed as her guardians for health as well as powers of attorneys. We convinced her to stay in the hospital until a place for her became available near the hospital. My mother admitted to me that she didn't believe that she had long left to live. She would never leave the hospital to live in a nearby hospice.

Hearing her talk about her death and realising that this was going to be my last chance to get answers, I again I tried to have her tell me the truth about the past, and again she refused and denied that there was anything that needed to be said. I knew that it was going to be the last time I would see her, just as I knew twenty-four years earlier when I was in Ottawa visiting my father that it was also a final visit. Both final visits left me forgiving and accepting these parents as they were at that time.

I returned home very frustrated and angry. I only had a few more weeks left at home in Canada before I would fly off to Toronto and then on to China for another year of teaching. In the days that remained before I flew off, those precious days when it was just the two of us, I found myself reconnecting with my inner self.

> *"In the swamplands of Mexico I somehow found my footing where nothing was visible from the surface, avoiding sinkholes and hidden dangers. In my dreams, the dream form of my ego, my sense of self seemed to know where to take the next steps forward regardless of the strange and often forbidding landscapes. When confronted with a mountain barrier or an ocean, I simply flew through the mountain or through the depths of the sea without fear. And in all of these scenes I am naked, unclothed. There are no masks, no costumes, no mirrors to distract or distort. In these scenes, the hidden self, the essential me is seen."* [August 11, 2011]

I spent ten days in Toronto before my wife joined me. I took care of our youngest grandson who was too ill to attend daycare while his parents worked. I took advantage of the extra time with him while waiting for my wife's flight to arrive. With her arrival in Toronto, we got to celebrate her birthday and then our anniversary before flying off to China for what would prove to be the last term of teaching in Changzhou.

Chapter Twenty-Six

The return to Changzhou saw me more focused that I had any right to expect. The preparation of documents needed by the university, especially the term plans, as well as a good start on lesson plans that would be needed for each of our classes were less of a challenge than in the past. I had put in enough time to know what was needed. As we met with the other expat teachers, new to the university, and the cooperating Chinese teachers I was given a lot of respect. I was the oldest instructor at the university with thirty-five years of experience, with a good number of those years as an administrator. My age, my life-long profession, and perhaps my quiet and confident presence added to the reasons they held me in high esteem. It did my ego a lot of good.

It is against this backdrop of a positive return to China that a dream emerged that woke me in the early hours one week into our return:

> *"... I walk for what seems to be hours and watch as the background scene changes ... the water beside the road has forced the road to become a narrow, sandy path which presses closer ... I look ahead and see the golden, sandy trail disappearing into the distance ... I know I can't make it to the end of the trail as I will be too hungry and weak ... I sit down thinking I should turn back ... I resist that thought and go on ... the path gets too narrow and I sense I will fall off the path into the water so I get down on all fours and slowly crawl forward ... the trail disappears under the water and I lose sense of direction ... turning to look back, all I see is water ... there is no way to go back and I don't know the way forward ..."* [September 6, 2011]

I was entering a strange place in my head. On my naturist blog site, I had begun to post conversations between my ego and my shadow, the ego clothed and the shadow stripped bare. The shadow was challenging my ego to be honest, to stop hiding and pretending and deflecting. The boundaries between my ego and the outer world and inner world were slowly disappearing. It seemed only a matter of time before I would find myself lost in both worlds.

As I continued my blogging, I found that I was engaging more often in a process of active imagination, a type of psychotherapy that enables bringing the unconscious world to the edge of one's awareness while one is awake. It is as if the brain creates a dream state. During this time, my Jungian Lens blog posts talked of active imagination, while in the Naturist Lens blog posts engaged in using active imagination.

> *"... one doesn't engage in active imagination to escape unpleasant realities. One uses active imagination to when most of the work of life in the outer world has been accomplished."* [September, 16, 2011]

The problem with all of this was, I hadn't yet finished taking care of the issues I had within the outer world. I still didn't know what all of those issues were even though I was sixty-two years old.

The practice of meditation I had begun in the previous spring continued. Since we had different instruction times, I typically would meditate while my wife was in class. I continued to meditate while nude, with gentle music playing in the background, usually mediation music, and sometimes with the sounds of Gregorian chant filling the silence. I used music in order to attempt to tame my mind in mediation. I described, in my journal the value and need for both blogging and meditation:

> *"I notice that my blogging is a ritual, a practice I engage in to honour my journey and to light the path on this journey. For me, blogging, is daring to step into ideas and paths that lead me out of my comfort zone of what I know. Blogging as a ritual. It seems to me that the paths of rituals are endless. Silent meditation is one path that I have used and will continue to use though the form of meditation seems to change. Sometimes the meditation is active such as in wandering with the camera. Sometimes the meditation is passive as in sitting still with music or incense or simply with a quiet centre."* [September 19, 2011]

The truth was that I had begun to find myself more agitated and emotionally unstable when time and circumstance got in the way of my blogging and meditation.

As September, 2011 came to an end, I found shadows shifting within me. At the time I had no idea what served as catalyst for this shift into depression and lethargy. Looking back into my journal I now can see that it had timed itself to match with messages and phone calls from my brother about our mother. She was giving up on life and was talking about quitting dialysis. Over the next month our communications became more frequent and frantic as we extended the conversations to include our other siblings. I tried to coax them into visiting our mother before her death. And, I began to slip behind in the process of preparing lessons for both of us. I soon turned to recycling my old lessons.

With the preoccupation with classes and the state of affairs with my mother, we didn't go for an exploration of a new part of China during the National Holiday. Rather, we spent the time walking around Changzhou visiting our favourite places and taking some needed time to catch up on course documentation and planning. The woman who was in charge of all foreign teachers had invited us to tour a park with her, her husband, and daughter. This family had become our closest Chinese friends and they wanted to share time together while their daughter was home from university classes which she took in a different city. We had eaten in each other's homes, toured together, worked together and often laughed together.

But, perhaps the most important part was that being with them removed us from being alone too much together. In my journal, a few days after our time with these friends I wrote:

> "*I wonder if our relationship is about dysfunction. Our life together is inclusive about almost everything. We are basically seen as inseparable; I have changed in significant ways and she has changed in significant ways. In spite of our enmeshed behaviours visible to the outer world, we are separate beings, at times almost strangers to each other. We have to tread gently when confronting these differences, but*

often the "treading on egg shells" aggravates old wounds, our open sores." [October 5, 2011]

Our night storms had begun to return and their intensity was frightening. I was once again finding myself punching myself in the head trying to drown out the fear and anger that I had caused to surface in my wife.

Just as the week of holidays came to an end, my mother married her consort of thirty-three years. They got married in the hospital where she was confined because of her health while taking dialysis treatments. My response was of relief and of anger that it had taken them so long to make their union official. The arguments between his children and our family had been bitter as there was no recognition of our mother as his life partner. The issue had always been about money and his will and his property. Now, that issue was set to rest. Our mother was now fully protected by law should anything happen to her husband.

I was angry because it was my mother who had refused to be married all those years. She needed to believe in her independence. There was no question, something deep was stirring within me that centred on my mother. A number of days after their wedding, while walking through a park where I saw a mother with her son of about ten years of age, a scene which I captured in a photograph, I wrote on my Jungian Lens blog site:

> *"I have been thinking of my own mother of late because of serious issues surrounding her health. My mother is 79. I don't really want to tell a tale of my mother in my own life as the tale would not really be adequate. There are too many little stories, scenes, poses and vignettes which would need to be presented and then there would still be huge holes in the tale. The mother I experienced and the mother experienced by each of my brothers and sisters is not the same. We each have left our childhood years with different images and associations with the word mother."* [October 18, 2011]

While all of this was going on, I began to take a series of on-line courses on Jungian psychology. I was once again running away from something lurking beneath the surface and hoping that, by focusing on these new courses while teaching and blogging and meditation, the hungry ghosts bubbling beneath the surface would retreat into the depths where they belonged. And then I bought a guitar and began to play it hoping that it would be enough to bring me peaceful silence.

A decision was made to take a break from teaching by both of us, a needed break from the routines of life in Changzhou. We thought that spending a week in the Philippines for sunshine, warmth, and snorkelling in the sea would be a good diversion for both of us. A rearrangement of our classes was approved by the university. As long as we gave our students the instructional time we were contracted for, there would be no problems with the university. Now that we were in our fourth year, we had earned a lot of trust with the university. We both needed to lay back in sunshine, to snorkel, and to enjoy a week of warmth.

Waiting. That is what my life had become as I worked my classes. It had seemed that the time for travelling to the Philippines would never come. I was stuck, very stuck. In my journal I wrote:

> *"Sometimes each day begins to morph into other days, almost featureless and not worth remembering. I seem to want more than "waiting" for something as time slips away. Since we all have a limited number of days and hours to live, I wonder at the pointlessness of some of these days and hours. At times like these, even reading or listening to anything that has depth is avoided as much as possible. I find myself engaged in mindlessness, activities such as playing solitaire against a computer. And noticing my "wasting" of time I get angry with myself, telling myself that I should know better."*
> [November 2, 2011]

Finally the time to leave for Moalboal on Cebu Island in the Philippines arrived. We had stretched our time to include two weekends so that we would have nine days away. We left after classes on Thursday to spend the night in Shanghai with our flight out the next morning. The blog post from Moalboal the next day was pregnant with dark premonitions of what was waiting:

"I am sitting on my balcony in a little beach resort in Moalboal, Philippines. I had visions of an isolated set of cottages along a mostly deserted beach, an expectation that faded quickly with the first look at the site and then taking a short walk along the beach. I was both disappointed and angry. Yet, in a way, I was almost expecting to be let down. I spent the night before flying out in Shanghai at the airport hotel with my room number being 6661. My first response was of shock – 666 was the sign of the devil. I immediately took that to mean that my unconscious was about to burst out of its container and make life miserable for me, leaving a trail of wreckage which I would then have to clean up."
[November 12, 2011]

In spite of my initial response, the beach, the villa, and the sea were a beautiful and welcome change from the damp cold that chilled us through to our bones in Changzhou. It didn't take long before I was out taking photos with my wife, discovering the shorelines, the nearby roads, and sunsets. We sat back and relaxed and breathed deeply and finally smiled at each other, happy to be in such a beautiful, warm place together.

Chapter Twenty-Seven

Two days after our arrival in the Philippines, November 14, 2011, my mother died. Several days later, I was finally able to write:

> *"I have to admit that I haven't been doing as well as I thought since the day my mother died. I had thought that I was prepared for her death knowing that it was coming and having had a week-long visit with her in order to say our good-byes. It took four days for the tears to finally come and allow the pressure to ease up.*
>
> *I descended into a darkness. I felt an intense guilt about still being alive even though it seemed a part of me had died; it was almost as if the creative inner force within me, my very soul had died. I wanted to disappear, forever, into that darkness. I was forgetting to breathe. A vise had seized my lower stomach and was squeezing for all it was worth and all I wanted was for it to stop, for stop to the pressure and pain."*
> [November 17, 2011]

I took refuge in meditation, nude as had become my practice. I meditated in the morning on our upper deck, and again later in the day in a secluded location along the beach. What had been planned as a holiday had become a time for grieving. As the eldest of her children, I tried to communicate to all of my brothers and sisters, and all of my mother's surviving family to let them all know. I set up an on-line memorial page so that the extended family spread across most of Canada could meet together, virtually in order to share their stories of her. And, in quiet moments I cried. Through all of this, my wife became my strength, my reason to keep breathing.

As I descended into despair over the next few days, it seemed that there were only two things that kept me afloat. The first was a retreat into naturism as I had done following the sexual abuse by my maternal grandfather. I needed to have control. I didn't have control over my mind and my feelings, but I did have control over my body. The second was my wife. She didn't criticise my increased time for nakedness, she validated it by taking photos of my meditation in nature. She pulled me forward to explore the edges of the sea and the edges of civilisation in the surrounding areas. She sat with me, beside me, as I mourned. And then we returned to Changzhou and the life of teaching in China.

Back in China, I still found the questions hounding me for answers, with the darkness pressing in. It seemed, somehow, as if there was something much larger and darker that the death of my mother and natural mourning going on behind the shell that was my head. In my journal, I wrote:

> *"Now that the children have homes of their own, I find that I have been travelling again, changing postal addresses though not at the same speed as I did as a youth. More than the changing of addresses was the return to unsettledness, the gypsy state of spirit. Changing locations in Canada, and including Mexico, Costa Rica, and China did not really allow me to find what was missing in being "here," being "present." Visiting countries hoping for a light to turn on didn't do it either. I only learned that the world was big and filled with people and that despite all the differences in climate and culture, there were more similarities than differences. I am learning that the answer isn't out there, somewhere. The answers that I seek are "here," within me.*
> [November 23, 2011]

The answers are to be found within, yet the darkness is also there. And so, like always, I kept my distance as much as possible and lived on in the outer world doing what I did best. Teaching.

The lessons went well, almost inspired lessons as I set aside expectations of what "should" be done, for what was more enlivening for my students. Their efforts and response again told me that I was a master at this craft of teaching. However, what I gave to them I refused, or couldn't give to myself. Rather, I buried myself in the words of others hoping to find answers that weren't there to be found.

November eased into December and life became quieter and less busy with the final classes made up and the annual round of Christmas activities yet to begin. I began to read a new book that I had carried with me on recommendation by my wife, who had already read it, a book called <u>Fire and Irises</u>. In the pages of Nicol's book I heard so many echoes.

> *"From the outside I suppose I looked as though I was fairly 'together.' I was a psychologist and held a full-time job, which I did adequately. But that was the cover story. I despaired that I would never be normal and wake up feeling happy like other people."*[14]

These words could have been written by me. In all likelihood they had been written by me over and over again over the years since the initial slips into depression that came with the approach of midlife. It didn't take me long to read the book.

Because of the guitar I had purchased, I found myself conscripted to perform in the university's Christmas concert which was mostly a performance of various Chinese songs and modern dance moves by university students. I was also cast in the role of Santa Claus with the task of giving out the treats to the students who gathered in the auditorium that seated a good portion of the campus where I taught. I sang, "The Angels Cried" as I just couldn't find it within me to sing some cheery song about Christmas, or snowmen, or wonderlands of snow.

When the concert was done, I took my guitar to my classes for a round of classroom Christmas activities. My will to do the work to create and deliver meaningful lessons had strangely vanished.

On Christmas Day, 2011, a sunny and warm day, we had taken a walk to the Metro store in order to buy some "foreigner" food and to stock up on Chilean wine as we had company coming for an evening meal. With the groceries bought and our backpacks filled with them, we began the half-hour walk back to our apartment. I had only managed to make it to the edge of the Metro parking lot when I stopped and sat down in a state of shock. I had had a flashback.

---

[14] Nicol, Fire and Irises, p. 34

I was assaulted by image after image from the past, images of sexual involvement with my mother. The woman I had honoured only a month earlier had been a sexual predator. Scenes with me at the age of ten were the first to emerge with what seemed like a deliberate attempt to have me return to her womb, images of me suffocating with my face pressed into her womb. I was terrified. Was this real? Was I making it up? Was this the ultimate betrayal of my mother? Or, was it the sacrifice of her son to her own darkness? It was the beginning of ongoing nightmares and flashbacks which would have me wake in the middle of the night, screaming and lashing out with my fists in an attempt to protect myself from the monsters hiding in my dreams.

As the end of term approached, before our departure for a term break holiday in Thailand, I found myself once again scrambling for marks and documentation that had marked my professional life before my breakdown in 1998. I was sinking, and sinking too fast. We both hoped that holiday time in the warmth and sunshine of Thailand would give me enough time to regain my ability to navigate the world of teaching at the university. We already both knew that this was going to be our last year in China. We just didn't know how it would all end.

Chapter Twenty-Eight

We arrived in Thailand on January 9, 2012. The warmth and the late afternoon sun felt like heaven after the damp, penetrating cold of Changzhou. It didn't take me long to begin taking photos. Our condo was large enough to give us a sense of space with its European elegance. I began to feel hopeful that this was just what I was needed in order to continue the work I had begun with the retelling of my history.

I continued to meditate finding a perfect location on a small balcony where I could soak in the sunshine while nude. We both took the time to go for our usual long walks in order to explore the community of Pattaya. In the other hours of the day, when we were not walking, I would turn to writing my history. I took occasional breaks so that we could spend time beside the swimming pool. I began to breathe a lot easier; life was again calming down.

However, it didn't take very many days before new flashbacks to appear. The intensity of those scenes were reflected in the nightmares that rattled both of us.

> *"Each time I dive into the unconscious, usually as a somewhat unwilling participant, doubtful and dubious of what is going to happen, I seem to suffer with the exposure of some inner darkness I wish didn't exist, an inner darkness that I hope is nothing but a figment of my imagination – 'Did this really happen, or am I making it up?' sort of darkness coming to light. Once exposed to the light I have a few choices; well, not really. I can own up to the facts, the moods, the events, the shit exposed and do it without laying blame, refusing to take the role of victim; or, I can deny, deny, deny; or, I can justifiably lay blame and become a victim thus relieving myself of any personal responsibility for becoming a better person, for healing myself."* [January 12, 2012]

I didn't retreat from the process of self-analysis. I was tired of being a victim, of not having any control. Besides, I had a significant background in psychotherapy which I believed would assist me in the process, as long as I kept one part of myself separate as an observer on the sidelines ready to intervene when the going got too rough or appeared to be getting out of control. The flashbacks and nightmares continued to assault me without regard for my skills and abilities as a mental-health counsellor.

In desperation knowing that I needed to consult an expert, on January 20th, I sent an e-mail to ZM in Canada asking him to consider taking me on as an analysand. I had gone too deep, had become too enmeshed with the shadows within me. I had lost my ability to gain control from the sidelines. I told my wife about my intentions of returning to analysis in Calgary rather than returning to Changzhou to finish off the last term. She was torn between keeping her word, her contract, and following me back to Canada. Her first response was to honour her contract thinking that I would respond as I had always responded, by accepting her choice and postponing the return to analysis. Whatever was happening to me and my needs to 'fix' myself was nothing new.

Yet, in spite of my old habit of giving in to meet her choices, I held firm to my intentions and told her that I would go to Canada while she finished off her contract. We would be together again in the summer when she returned to Canada. With my decision made, she sent in our resignations to the university. My defence of my choice rang true in her ears and she agreed to go back home with me to Canada. We then began the search for a place to live in Calgary.

In spite of the chaos reigning within me, I continued to be my own analyst, continued to wander the depths and the shadows. The decision to go into analysis gave me renewed courage and hope. My journal records the process:

> *"The process has me risking self-analysis, taking myself on as a patient, watching the process from the sidelines and recording data and then daring to ask my 'self' some tough questions about what my 'self' has said and seen. If this sounds a bit like 'dissociation, it is. Dissociation is at work, but it has always been at work to some extent for as long as I can remember, probably all the way back to my early childhood."* [January 25, 2012]

Then, my journal went quiet as I walked with my wife, read, took a few photos of people and places, and took skyclad meditative moments. She had come to understand better what was going on within me.

> *"Each day while I am engaged in my early morning nude meditation, M goes jogging. Each morning, she has returned from her jog with a flower that has fallen from some tree as a gift to me, a promise that through the process of healing, we are in it together."* [February 2, 2012]

The last weeks in Pattaya, Thailand were quieter and gentler between the two of us. She followed as I wandered with camera in hand through the edges of community, discovering several Buddhist temples for us to explore. Buddhism was showing me a psychological face that had fit with what I understood about being human. I was trying to understand about always feeling alone in spite of being surrounded by people who loved and respected me. And in this search for more answers, I began to read again about Buddhism.

The return to Changzhou in order to pack up our lives was not easy for either of us. How could we explain to our friends and colleagues there that we were leaving with a job half done? The simplest answer seemed to be a blend of the truth with some poetic license: I had cancer of the brain. People understood cancer and accepted it as a sad reality. However, there is difficulty in understanding that the brain has collapsed under the weight of darkness leaving a person balanced between life and death. As we packed during those last five days in Changzhou, I took to slipping into positive memories from the past, memories of the first years with my wife. There was no energy left within me for self-analysis. I needed to retreat into safer inner spaces while waiting to make the transition back into the safety net of psychoanalysis.

Chapter Twenty-Nine

"I realise that even though I am home in Canada, I am 'un étranger.' We are all strangers even within our own families and communities, even if we have never left our home communities. In truth, we are strangers to ourselves." [February 16, 2012]

We stopped in Toronto to spend a few days with our son and his young family before flying home to Saskatchewan. The few days in Toronto renewed my belief in family as I saw my son, his wife, and son actively engaged in their new life, in a new home. In this setting, I looked at my wife and knew what she had sacrificed and endured in our relationship because she loved me. She had been on this journey before in 1998, a journey that had ended up with her giving up a home and career in order to go where I needed to go once that process of analysis was done. Again, she had given up another career she loved because it was what I needed. But what did she need? I could only guess that she needed to be with me, to be beside me. She had invested more than forty years in our marriage and was not going to quit. I saw that in Toronto and wrote in my Jungian Lens blog site:

> *"Like me, she has to hold the tension, waiting and hoping that this time the process will do what it needs to do in order to allow her to have her life back. And it is there that I finally understand something important. Her life, similar to my life, is one that is only whole in relationship. The loss of relationship would be the greatest loss. Embracing relationship as whole individuals, even as broken individuals, is what animates us."* [February 19, 2012]

On February 24th, I had my first session with ZM. I had woken up that morning before dawn to sit still in the living room of the basement suite we had rented in Calgary. I took a photo of the dawn. The sky appeared to be on fire, red fire. I thought of the old expression, "Red sky in the morning, sailors take warning." And that made me worry about just what the hell had I was unleashing by this move back into Jungian analysis. I was worried that somehow I was going to screw it all up, that the analyst was going to find me wanting and would refuse to work with me. I wondered if I would be able to give the right answers to his questions, I was worried that I would become too silent and hide behind meaningless words because I was too ashamed. ZM already knew quite a bit about me, but he set that aside in order to do the foundational work of building a safe place for the analytical work to happen. Without that foundation, the analytic process would fail. The journey of healing had begun again, the journey which had begun fourteen years earlier in the same city.

Journey of a Wounded Healer

Sitting in my rocking chair
Surrounded by the darkness of the night
Imagining the horrors that have no name
Tears well for no reason other than as a protest.

Sitting in my rocking chair locked in the silence of night
Fearing the horrors that have no name
Fighting for strength in the light of a new day
Breathing deeply to contain the terror of an unknown future.

Eyes strained from sleeplessness and tenseness
Fighting for hope in the promise of a new day
Closing my eyes to contain the terror of an unknown future
The wounded healer's journey begins.
[December 15, 1997]

The journey began and I struggled in spite of having my wife beside me all the moments when I wasn't in analysis. It got harder and harder to navigate the hours in between sessions. I tried desperately to be a partner for her, to share normal life and do normal things with her. She deserved at least that much. I felt guilty for not being present enough though I was physically beside her. My nightmares woke her and we would lay beside each other worried about each other and ourselves.

Reaching back into my past, I knew I needed to devote a lot more of my healing time to solitary silence. I knew that in addition to that solitude, I needed to meditate, to draw, to write and to play music.

While I began to meet these needs, my wife would make journeys to see her brothers in Lethbridge while I worked on my sanity. A new guitar was purchased as my old one too damaged to play anymore. I had hoped that music would be yet another tool to aid in my journey.

I also began to attend Buddhist meditation evenings in hopes that by learning more formally about Buddhism, I could build a better foundation for my meditation practice, for my psyche. Each week took me deeper into the mysteries of Tibetan Buddhism which seemed to help me navigate the days that slowly made their way towards spring.

Two months into analysis, I asked my wife to return to our home, to leave me in Calgary and to trust in me to work through the process. I would make the journey back to our home, as I had done fourteen years earlier. I needed the space in which to fall apart without having to see the pain that it caused in her. I needed to invest my energies in the process and not worry about failing to be present enough with her. I sent her home and felt like a traitor to our relationship. She had given up her teaching and followed me and now it was as if I was rejecting her. I didn't know how to explain to her that I wasn't rejecting her, I was trying to stop rejecting myself, stop denying myself the full attention to healing that I needed. I wanted to heal and be with her as a mentally healthy man finally ready to be a good husband.

The storm that erupted with my decision, like so many storms in the past, had me turn on myself destructively. I deleted the naturist blog site, deleted my journal, and deleted many photos of myself from our photo archives. I simply wanted it all to end. And as so often in the past, I struck out at her by punching myself in the head. Yet, it wasn't her I was trying to punish, it was my mother who had raped me. And, I was punishing myself for the shame of allowing so many others including my mother to sexually abuse me.

I didn't see myself as a man who deserved to have a wife. I believed the criticisms of me for not having the balls to stand up for myself. Yet this was exactly what I had just done, I had stood up for myself. Yet, for all of that, I would have backed down if she would have pressed me.

There was a lot of anger, a lot of tears when that decision was made. But, that decision had provided the momentum for me to get unstuck from the quagmire. That decision was followed up with a dream that spoke of hope.

> *". . . We have bought a house package and we will be putting it on our lot in place of our old house . . . I am at a loss o how this will work . . . can we build the new house first while still living in the old house? . . . we are in having problems with the old house and I find myself outside with her looking for answers to questions . . . there is a man who points to a rail track, one wide, single rail. . . I check out how it is supposed to work and see that begins with a rise that has a small drop-off that allows for an initial speed to carry the load smoothly and easily forward . . . I am still wondering about the house and where it will go in the yard . . . as I am about ready to go back into the old house . . . I notice her come out of the house with our last child . . . as usual they are nude as I am . . . I go into the house and find the house plans on the bed, just what I was looking for . . . she left them there for me and she left a love note with the plans . . . I look at the plans noting the dimensions . . . I return outside and look for a tape measure so that I can ascertain the position of the house . . . in the garage which transforms itself into a deck, the new plants in their new pots/bowls are being unpacked by her and a man . . . he shows us how the plants are self-watering . . . the self-watering feature leaves a lot of water on the deck surface and I am just about to let them know that this system is messy when the plants tilt sideways in their pots so that a blast of warm drying air can clean up the excess water . . . strange is all that I can think . . . the process needs to be re-designed to work out the bugs in the system . . . I still don't know if the house will fit . . . I think of moving the house very close to the property line and having a very high privacy fence . . ."* [April 22, 2012]

The outer world of our relationship had painted a different image than the dream. If anything, it looked as though our marriage was approaching a time of endings. Yet, the dream told me a different story, one that I trusted and clung to as if it was an anchor as I was being tossed by storm winds on a sea.

At the beginning of May, I moved from the house we had lived in together while in Calgary. I had found a smaller and less expensive basement suite in a different location, one that was closer to the analyst's office. I was officially on my own, in my own suite, very alone. I took refuge in Buddhism, played my new guitar, wrote dreams, wrote blog posts, walked and walked, took an occasional photo, and waited to see where analysis was going to take me.

I was putting all of my bets on analysis and my meditation practice to bring me back to health. However, in the process, I forgot about taking care of my body. The stresses of analysis weren't countered by any conscious attention to my eating habits. I ignored the need for proper rest. As a result, my weight soared along with my blood pressure. I had only found this out when I went to a fitness gym and got an evaluation which would then lead to a tailored fitness plan. My blood pressure was too high for the fitness consultant. I needed to get clearance from a doctor before I could begin.

And so, I went to the doctor who confirmed the high blood pressure and I was placed on medications. I began to walk seriously. My diet changed as well. I walked for hours at a time focusing on pace and distance as I once had when I had trained for marathons. My goal was to simply find a way to get well in body, mind and spirit.

> *"It's been almost three months since I have returned to analysis, to the work of diving deep into the darkness of an inner world in order to reconnect and remember. Now, there seems to be a sense that the light is beginning to rekindle external life with a new sense of energy and urgency, an upwelling of libido which demands that I live fully in my body as well as in my head. Yes, there is an urgency in this as the years of my life are racing towards a return to the source of all being. I am being told, 'don't sit back and wait for a better time, for this is the time, now!'* [May 20, 2012]

As analysis progressed with me living in Calgary and my wife living back in our home in Saskatchewan, I would make my way back to our home every second week-end to be with her. We returned to the pattern we had lived fourteen years earlier. As in the past, the journey between Calgary and our home was difficult, especially the return trip back to Calgary.

Time apart for my analysis wasn't working as well as it had in the past. There was a sense that I would have to make a choice between a new life that included on-going analysis with the likelihood of becoming an analyst myself; or a return home with the risks of again breaking down and causing all sorts of suffering for my wife and others. This often became a focus of the analytical sessions which seemed to point to my becoming an analyst in the Calgary area. My analyst encouraged me to follow this old dream that dated back twenty years to a time before my first series of Jungian analysis. I couldn't move from being stuck between these opposite poles as it basically came down to life with or without my wife.

Each week I continued to visit the Marpa Gompa Buddhist centre and immersed myself in Buddhist ideas. I would go early to the centre so that I could walk around the area before the meditation sessions. At times I would go to the local Starbucks for coffee and read Buddhist books. The more I read about Tibetan Buddhism, the more I found resonances within myself. There were also resonances with what I understood about Jungian psychology. Near the end of May 2012, I began to read a new book by Trungpa called, Smile at Fear.

> *"We also have to give up the notion of a divine savior, which has nothing to do with what religion we belong to, but refers to the idea of someone or something who will save us without our having to go through any pain ... If you are really interested in working with yourself, you can't lead that kind of double life, adopting ideas, techniques, and concepts of all kinds simply in order to get away from yourself ... Nobody can save you from yourself."*[15]

I heard the same words that had been already said many times by my wife, my analyst, and by others I had met along the way. It appeared

---

[15] Trungpa, Smile at Fear, pp 5-6

that I was finally ready to really hear these words. I had to own my physical health and my mental health. I had no choice but to begin to own it all.

The shift of focus to include my body was matched by a new vision, to walk the Camino de Santiago. I had envisioned making the walk a three-month long journey leaving from either Paris or Le Puy en Velay. After doing a lot of research from a variety of online sources, I decided that Le Puy would be my starting point.

With the vow to walk the Camino, I realized that this would require a break in analysis. For a while, I kept my vow to myself without mentioning it to ZM, my analyst. First, I had wanted to see if my body would be strong enough for that pilgrimage, especially after receiving the poor results about my blood pressure.

My body responded well and I found myself walking to and from analysis when the weather was cooperative, a round trip that was about fourteen kilometres. I then bought new shoes and a few other hiking essentials for the Camino.

In June, I took two weeks off from analysis while ZM went for a holiday in Europe. I returned home for those two weeks. I meditated, and did some golfing with our friends. We spent quiet time together and I read. For those two weeks my life once again felt normal.

It wasn't long after my return to Calgary in order to resume analysis that I watched a movie called 'The Way.' I sent a message to my wife to have her watch the movie. The movie had reinforced my vow of walking the Camino; and, it allowed me to feel brave enough to let both my wife and ZM know about my intention to walk the Camino. My analyst was confused as to why I would do this, especially since we still had a lot of work to do together. And my wife simply stayed quiet not ready to believe it to be more than another meaningless resolve.

Analysis continued as if my intention was had never been mentioned. ZM had given me encouragement to return to schooling for a Master of Counselling Psychology degree which would then be the launching pad for me to enter into analytical training at a Jungian institute. ZM made this assumption believing I would leave my marriage. I said little in response, and said even less about my Camino plans. It began to feel to me as if we were not walking the journey of analytical work together – he was leading one direction and I was taking a fork in the road, away from being a Jungian analyst.

Every trip back home taught me that my life there was more authentic. It was then that I began to believe that ZM saw me as following in his footsteps. I wanted my own footsteps and those footsteps were on a life path that included my wife. I only saw her in my future.

Chapter Thirty

In late June, I was sitting on the back deck at home reading. What I had just read illustrated perfectly the life I had been living. It was then that I told my wife of my not returning to Calgary and analysis. She asked me "Why?" and I told her that to continue in analysis would end up in our never being able to come back together again. Continuing analysis was a one-way street to a future without her in it, a future I didn't want. I told her again about my plans to walk the Camino that fall and that I would leave the day after our wedding anniversary.

With my return to Calgary in the first week of July, I returned to my last set of analytical sessions with ZM. The shift which had happened within me, was sending me on a pilgrimage in search of healing and forgiveness. I needed to feel it in my body, this forgiveness of myself and all of those who had abused me in my past. I had to forgive myself.

Those final two weeks in Calgary, I hiked with determination, a passion to push myself to the point of exhaustion. Analysis became just something I did in the background when I wasn't walking, reading and writing, doing meditation, and simply being alone with myself. Though I hadn't taken my first step on the Camino path, I had effectively already become a pilgrim.

> *"The particular reasons which drive an individual towards an act of pilgrimage are inevitably deeply personal, and in many cases beyond the exercise of logic alone. Even though the physical dangers are not as great as they once were, the psychological and spiritual ferment remains. Those who are close to the pilgrim may well ask why they have undertaken such an action. The act of pilgrimage disturbs the lives of those who surround the pilgrim."*[16]

Disturbing the lives of others was something I hadn't thought of very much. Rather, my intention was to disturb and banish the ghosts of my past so that they would leave me alone. Already, though the

[16] Robinson, Pilgrim Paths: An Anthology of Pilgrimage

pilgrimage was a month and a half away, I could feel my body respond to the deliberate stresses of training. My meditation practice became deeper in response, my ego became stronger. I knew that I was finding the necessary will power to break out of dependence on others and the dependence on analysis. This was the whole point of going into analysis in the first place.

On my last weekend in Calgary, I went into the nearby mountains by Canmore to challenge myself with physical ascents and descents. I climbed a path I had never been able to climb in the past when we had visited the same place. I had to confront my fear of heights on my own. I walked on the edge of an abyss as I climbed the path. It made me think of old stories I had read as a youth, stories from the Lives of the Saints where those on their spiritual quests often punished themselves, pushed their limits in search of meaning and connection with their chosen God. Like me, these ancients had searched for something to fill the holes in their hearts and minds. They were pilgrims of a different sort on their own journeys of healing, a journey that I had re-entered when I chose to stop teaching in China, and do the hard work to claim my body, mind, and spirit as my own.

> *"Almost everyone who undertakes a true spiritual path will discover that a profound personal healing is necessary part of his or her spiritual process. When this need is acknowledged, spiritual practice can be directed to bring such a healing to body, heart, and mind. This is not a new notion. Since ancient times, spiritual practice has been described as a process of healing."[17]*

I left Calgary after having told ZM of my intentions for not returning, at least not until I had finished walking the Camino. Yet, I wasn't so certain about that when I left his office. Questions such as, 'What if I changed my mind after a few days at home, realizing that I wasn't really ready to leave the safety of analysis?' made me have doubts. In spite of the doubts, I gave him notice.

---

[17] Kornfield, A Path With Heart, p. 40

"Things falling apart is a kind of testing and also a kind of healing. We think that the point is to pass the test or to overcome the problem, but the truth is that things don't really get solved. They come together and they fall apart. Then they come together again and fall apart again. It's just like that. The healing comes from letting there be room for all of this to happen ..."[18]

I set aside blogging at the Jungian Lens site. I set up a new blog site for the Camino. In spite of that intention, the new blog site was only up for a few weeks after it was born. I then deleted it. I just couldn't find the will to write up blog posts as if I was celebrating a new adventure.

Rather than write, I spent my time with my wife who was suffering in advance of my departure to Europe. We golfed together, we sat still together, we cried together, and we both worried at what the future had in store for us as a couple. At the end of July, I let our children know about my Camino plans. And then, just days before their arrival at our home, I wrote:

"So why am I doing this? Well, it is what I consider to be the next, and hopefully second last part of my healing process. The last part of the process is coming home and staying there with Mom without being tortured by the demons of my childhood past. This walk is taking place so that I can "walk the Devil out of me." I have, like all people, hurt and scarred people as I moved through life, including in various ways, each of you. And like almost all people, I didn't even know I was leaving a trail of hurt behind me. We hurt each other and we hurt ourselves in spite of our best intentions. So, the journey is one of seeking absolution, a forgiveness of my "transgressions," as well as a forgiveness for those who "transgressed against" me. That is a very "Catholic" belief. As you know, I have also included Buddhism into my belief system, something that I am finding more and more vital to my sanity. It is teaching me about being at peace with myself. So, as well as praying on this journey, I will take time to

---

18 Chodron, When Things Fall Apart, p. 8

meditate. Between the two, I will, repeat - will - find the inner peace that has been missing for so long. That is the gift I will be bringing home - being a peace with myself so that both Mom and I can enjoy the last twenty to thirty years of our life together." [August 6, 2012]

Everyone came home in August. I explained to them what I was going to do. With that said, almost everyone in the family simply accepted it as yet another step in their Papa's journey of healing. I also talked to them about going silent for the most part while I would be in Europe. I then took a photo of all of us which I intended on carrying with me on the Camino. When everyone had returned home, my son wrote to me, a small note that I hoped would be the real result of my pilgrimage:

"The upcoming silence will be the power that heals you. Keep an eye on the 'prize' and know we all love you and support you on this journey." [August 13, 2012]

As the days passed by at a lazy summer pace, I worried about the future fallout of my pilgrimage. The words of Martin Robinson came back and troubled me: *"The act of pilgrimage disturbs the lives of those who surround the pilgrim."* I might be doing the walking, but everyone else in my life was going to be affected, disturbed by my decision to walk. The ripples would flow out each and every day before I left, and continue to flow out during all the days that I would be gone from home. Each, in their own way, was taking a parallel journey that rippled out from my Camino. I wouldn't be alone. All of them would be there within me, and that made the decision to get on the plane and leave for Paris.

Chapter Thirty-One

"I am tired of running. I am worn out from running. I am tired of darkness and fear. It seems I can't run far enough or fast enough to get away from myself. The act of going on a pilgrimage is not about running away. It puts me into a place, space and time where I am forced with each step, each kilometre and each scene to be face-to-face with myself. It is about forcing myself to face the facts of who I am without being able to turn to you or our children or our grandchildren as a way to escape facing myself. I have to accept that it is hopeless for you or our children and grandchildren to fill the black holes, or to build a thick enough barrier to permanently bury them – hopeless. I need to be able to turn to myself, to make friends with myself, to trust myself. I know I can't do this at home as the moment I look up and see you, I am undone, falling into the cocoon of you. I see you, my magical other, and avoid looking at me.

Going on this pilgrimage is about love in a big way. If I return able to be my own friend, trusting myself; I will be able to love you more as an equal. You are not my mother and I need to stop giving you a mother's authority over me. It's not about what you do or what you have done; it is about what I do and what I have done or not done. So, I go on this pilgrimage walking slowly, one step and one day at a time, to become friends with myself. This is not about running or escaping. I go so that when I return, you will find that your husband is a man, not a child trapped in a man's body. I go so that I can stop being afraid of both living and dying.

I want the next 30 or more years, to be years where we can laugh, play, travel, drink coffee, walk, golf, do all that will fill those years, as equal partners in love and life."
[August19, 2012]

The plane to Paris left on time. I arrived in Paris the next morning and made my way to my hostel in Montmartre just a few blocks from the Basilique Sacre Coeur. I planned on using my time until I left for Le Puy, in tracing the steps of pilgrims of the past who left from Paris to go to Santiago. I walked in the hot August afternoon from the Basilique Sacre Coeur to the Tour Saint Jacques. From there I went on to the Cathedral Notre Dame where I got my pilgrim's passport stamped. While in the Cathedral, I sat in a pew in silence with tears tracing lines down my cheeks. Why were there tears; and what were they about? I had no answers. Wiping my eyes, I then walked down Rue Saint Jacques to another church, Saint Jacques du Haut Pas, my last stop before making my way back to the hostel. I was hot, tired, and I already had blisters.

I was falling apart at the seams. I had never had problems when travelling, not even in China where language was a barrier. Yet, before I even left Paris, my carefully constructed plans fell apart. I found myself sitting in the wrong train at the station. I hadn't paid enough attention to realise that I was on the train that had arrived from Lyon, not the train that was going to Lyon. When the departure time came and went, I realised my mistake. I rushed back to the ticket office to see what I could do to get to Le Puy en Velay where I had booked a bed in a hostel for that night.

> *"When things fall apart and we're on the verge of we know not what, the test for each of us is to stay on that brink and not concretize. The spiritual journey is not about heaven and finally getting to a place that's really swell. In fact, that way of looking at things is what keeps us miserable . . . the only time we ever know what's really going on is when the rug's been pulled out and we can't find anywhere to land. We use these situations either to wake ourselves up or to put ourselves to sleep"[19]*

I finally woke up to the need to be present. There was no extra cost for new train tickets, except the cost to my pride. In spite of missing the first train, I wouldn't be late for the pilgrimage registration in Le Puy. I had a bed for the night. I knew I had to remain alert and fully awake. The journey to Le Puy went without further mishap as I navigated the change of trains in Lyon without mishap. I made it to the cathedral in Le Puy in time to register for the Camino.

---

[19] Chodron, When Things Fall Apart, p. 9

I attended the Pilgrim Mass the next morning where I got the bishop's blessing and began the anticipated journey.

I walked longer than I had planned for that first day. I walked passed my intended stop in Montbonnet and arrived at Saint Privat d'Allier totally exhausted. At the private hostel where I had stopped for the night, I was reluctant to join in the conversations of the others who had also walked from Le Puy. I kept to myself and began to imagine that the others were talking about me in negative terms. It was only when the majority of them had left to go to the local mass or to wander the town that I finally turned to meditation with the hopes of escaping a growing sense of paranoia within me. When it was time for the evening meal, the paranoia was gone. I finally began to interact with the other pilgrims and our hosts.

With the passing of each day I continued to walk further than I had originally planned. I stopped at intervals to sit alongside the path and to read from Pema Chodron's book, or to chart my journey in the Miam Miam guide book I had purchased in Paris. I walked with a determined purpose. I walked alone. The blisters I got in Paris became larger and walking became more and more difficult. I valued walking alone and in pain. It almost felt as though the blisters were what I needed and what I deserved.

> "*As I got ready to start the fourth day of walking, I noticed that I was approaching the coming walk with more confidence. If I had been at home I would have been checking with others to verify my choices, never really trusting myself to make the right choices. On the trail I was forced to make choices without turning to anyone else for at these times, there was no one else around, most times not even another pilgrim hobbling down the trail. More confidence. Even the pain in my feet was helping me. I was learning to cope better with adversity, even if that adversity was due to my choices. I was learning to dig deeper into my willpower to keep going in spite of pain, in spite of discouragement.*" [September 4, 2012]

Leaving Saugues the next morning I got lost in the pre-dawn light, I had to backtrack into town and search for the Camino trail. I was again reminded that I had to get out of my head and be where I was, or I was going to continue to get lost. It was this realisation that made me realise just what it was that the Camino was supposed to teach me; at least one of the lessons I needed to learn.

> *"This morning, I left a bit later than normal after sleeping in, following a night of poor sleep. There was a sense of guilt that plagued me as I lay in bed, guilt for finding that the day that had just passed was a good day. I felt guilty for enjoying the walk, for taking time to be present in an outer world, time to wander and take photographs. Somehow I believed that it was necessary to be depressed and miserable, to suffer and suffer some more. It wasn't enough that my feet and hips were hurting. I bought into the guilt and found ways to punish myself with my negative thoughts."* [September 6, 2012]

I still had all of my ghosts and the shadows to deal with; I had the guilt of not staying to care for my brothers and sisters while they were at the mercy of my parents; and I felt guilty for so many things I had done and for those things that had been done to me. In spite of a lesson learned, I had a long road ahead of me. I was still fighting nameless ghosts and shadows.

The next day began with fog, and the pilgrims in front of me became like the ghosts in my head. The silence of the fog pressed on me. As I walked across the eerie landscape of the Aubrac filled with large broken rocks, I came across a shelter. I entered the shelter that was shrouded with fog and found another pilgrim huddled within it. We talked together, we had seen each other earlier and he wondered if I was a Buddhist as he had seen me meditating in a hostel and along the side of the trail. He was a young German university student. I listened to his story and we became pilgrim friends.

The rest of the day's walk was done in a better mood which was matched by the fog lifting. We found ourselves sharing the same hostel where we decided to cook a communal meal later in the day. I then went wandering through the village and found the church.

"When I got to the town's cathedral, I soon found myself sitting along one of the sides, in the shadows, where again tears began to fall. Again I was ready to just quit the whole thing. But even thinking of quitting didn't help stem the tears as then I began to cry at the prospect of returning home and still being lost in my inner darkness. I knew that this was my last hope if I was to emerge sane, to emerge as a man who would be fit to be a husband, father, and grandfather. Finally I settled back into accepting that I would continue the pilgrimage and risk everything on a positive result. I knew I wasn't there yet." [September 6, 2012]

I had come so close to quitting, believing that I wasn't good enough to be a pilgrim. The following day was more encouraging as I walked to Espalion. It became a long day interspersed with reading from Chodron's book and meditations along the way.

On September 8th, the guilt returned to hound me. It seemed that Pema Chodron knew what to say in her book to trigger, to awaken the buried pain I had forgotten existed.

"This is how it actually works. There has to be some kind of respect for the jitters, some understanding of how our emotions have the power to run us around in circles. That understanding helps us discover how we increase our pain, how we increase our confusion, how we cause harm to ourselves." [September 8, 2012]

And then, surprisingly, I found my balance, I remembered why I was walking the Camino. It was the pain, the ghosts, the quest for healing so that I could be a better person for myself and those who loved me. I was walking to save my sanity and my soul.

Chapter Thirty-Two

The walk to Conques was filled with a strange need to hurry, I had a premonition that something important waited for me in Conques, something momentous. I arrived and was immediately disappointed with the Cathedral. The only thing I could think of was the pain in my feet as I struggled on the cobble stone streets and climbing the steep hills within the tiny town. I knew that it wasn't the cathedral that seemed to be missing its grandeur, but rather my expectations that had been growing during the day's walk. I took a few photos, then retreated to the municipal hostel where I showered, meditated, and then napped.

I woke after a short, fitful sleep upon hearing other pilgrims enter the hostel bedroom to claim their bunks. I had met quite a few of the original pilgrims whom I had met in Saint Privat d'Alliers, as well as a few others along the Camino. The group had intended to go back to the cathedral later in the evening for a presentation about the cathedral by the local priest, and I agreed to go with them.

As darkness filled the evening sky and with a simple meal finished, I went to the cathedral courtyard to meet with my pilgrim friends. For a few, this was the end of their journey. For most of the others, the journey would last another two days, and would end in Figeac. I was the only one in the group who had the intention of walking all the way to Santiago, Spain.

> *"The priest spoke well with a hint of humour in his presentation. While he was speaking, a man in his thirties appeared at the edges of the crowd. I immediately felt the hair rising on the back of my neck. I found myself dividing my attention between the priest and this man. As he wandered along the edges of the crowd, I could tell that he was looking for someone. Finally, he stopped and looked in my direction, but not at me. He was looking at a tall, blond woman near me, one of the original group from Saint Privat d'Alliers. When he saw her, his gave a big grin as he waved at her. However, his eyes didn't smile as if he had just found a friend. I knew immediately that he was a predator. So did the group around me.*

The priest went on with his story as if unaware of the predator in the crowd. As he told the tale of a young girl who came to be Sainte Foy, the predator moved closer, smiling at the blond then quickly turning his head to scowl as he surveyed the rest of the crowd. The blond moved closer to me as if I would protect her somehow. The priest began to ask questions which all had the same answer, Sainte Foy. As he asked the question, the predator was the one who gave the response. It didn't take me long to realise that the priest and the predator knew each other. The responses were too much like an altar boy's responses in a mass. I began to wonder how long this drama had been playing out, how many years had the predator prowled the edges of the crowd, giving the priest his needed answers while he searched for his next victim." [September 9, 2012

As the scene unfolded, I found myself cast into the role of protector by the women in the group. They had gathered around the woman who they felt was the chosen victim of the predator. I took on the role of protector without thinking. The man whom I had identified as a predator, withdrew when he saw my face and felt my eyes giving his a warning to stay away from the group. Finally as the evening ended with music in the Cathedral, everyone withdrew from the church leaving me alone in it. Tears began to fall. I was grieving my loss of innocence as a child. I was angry at the predators in the church who took advantage of their power when I was a young boy. And then, when the tears stopped flowing, I left the church and returned to the hostel.

"Once in my bunk, I decided to take some time to meditate. Curiously, sitting in my meditation with a focus on breathing, I began to loosen the tension in my body. I felt a sense of release from the darkness, as though the ghosts that had been in pursuit had finally given up the chase. And then, I slept."

The next day I was again filled with the need to hurry forward in spite of the blisters which were growing out of control. I hurried in hopes of finding a place where I could find an Internet café so that I could talk with my wife. Nothing else mattered for me. It had been too many days already since our last contact and I knew she would be frantic with worry about me. Yet for all the pressing on, the next village didn't have an Internet connection available for me to use.

In my journal, a book given to me by eldest daughter for the Camino, I wrote:

> *"I had lost the smile that I had found earlier that day on the trail. I again began to feel sorry for myself, angry at others. For a while in the morning I thought I finally had gotten it all together. And then, I read these words by Pema Chodron:*

> "To think that we can finally get it all together is unrealistic. To seek for some lasting security is futile. To undo our very ancient and very stuck patterns of mind requires that we begin to turn around some of most basic assumptions. Believing in a solid, separate self, continuing to seek pleasure and avoid pain, thinking that someone "out there" is to blame for our pain – one had to totally get fed up with these ways of thinking. One has to give up hope that this way of thinking will bring us satisfaction. Suffering begins to dissolve when we can question the belief or the hope that there's anywhere to hide. "

> *I was sad, losing hope and blaming the world. I wanted the walk to save me; I wanted M. to save me; I wanted analysis to save me. None of it was working. I blamed my parents, the priests who molested me, my grandfather. So many people had hurt me as I grew up, even as an adult. I wanted them all to somehow fix me, take responsibility for my depression, for my loss of hope, for the darkness that haunted me."*

The next morning, I walked on having slept badly. Somehow, in spite of the poor sleep, I felt a strange sense of being more at peace with myself. The only anxiety that remained was of being able to find an Internet connection so that I could let my wife and my children know that I was okay, perhaps even better than okay.

By the time I got to Figeac late in the afternoon, I knew I couldn't walk any further, my feet were in too much pain. Yet, rather than go to the hostel to rest, I wandered around the city in search of Internet.

I found Internet service in a computer store. I talked with my wife for more than an hour, even after the owner of the shop had closed his place for the evening. He had seen my tears as I entered messages to my wife, and he couldn't bear to interrupt."

> *Her: Where are you?*
> *me: I am in Figeac, ahead of my schedule*
> *Her: Ok. Expected an e-mail from Conques, so was so worried.*
> *me: If you promise to do the second half with me, the Spain part, I will go home when I finish the France part, in three more weeks.*
> *Her: I promise with all my heart.*
> *me: We could do it in two years from now*
> *Her: This is too hard apart. You decide when, I promise to come.*
> *me: I will plan when and where I will quit this lonely walk so that we can do it together.*
> *Her: Ok, quit tomorrow would be great for me, but I will wait for you, that I promise. I miss you more than life itself, but I want you to heal and decide what is best for you.*
> *me: It won't be long, believe me.* [September 11, 2012]

The next morning, I left the hostel early in search of answers as I wandered streets in the pale light of dawn. Eventually I found a tiny café where I ate a small breakfast. I sat in silence without being forced to talk with other pilgrims. Most of the pilgrims I had met were leaving the Camino and new ones to take their place. I had left the hostel without saying goodbyes to the pilgrims who had become friends on the trail. I sat and wondered if I was going on to walk the rest of the trail to Saint Jean Pied de Port. The time I spent in the café stretched longer than normal as I ordered more coffee. I had made my decision. My Camino in France was done. It was time to go home.

Chapter Thirty-Three

I returned home from France a changed man. I hadn't been healed; however, I had put a lot of ghosts to rest. I knew that a long and difficult journey still lay ahead. Another different kind of pilgrimage was yet I to be walked, one that would be shared. While I wrote about my pilgrimage in France, we planned for a winter of warmth in Central America. First we would have a short stay in Mexico followed by the remainder of our winter spent in Belize.

It didn't take me long to set up a meditation corner in my office, a sacred space which I began to use to retain a sense of balance. I returned to meditating nude in that sacred space. Nude meditation felt more honest, a complete immersion into a state of sacredness.

I felt my nudity challenge my belief systems as I bounced back and forth between the two extremes of wearing clothes and being clothing free. First there was too much nudity and then no nudity in our home. As it began to be evident that no nudity left me very agitated, my wife eased back on her expectations. Neither of us understood why I needed to be nude, but we both knew that life was better for both of us if my nudity was given its time and place in my life.

And so at this time, I began to take naturism seriously. And, as always when I decide to look at things in depth, I turned to Jungian psychology. It was the lens through which I hoped to come to grips with my compulsion for nudity.

> "*I intend on presenting a series of posts that look at alchemy from a naturist and psychological point of view. If I accept that naturism allows one to achieve a physical state that is in holistic balance with the earth, with relationship with others and with the self, it is desirable that one looks for psychological balance as well since we are as much spirit as we are body.*" [November 14, 2012]

It was the birth of a new blog site, Through a Naturist Lens that was twinned with Through a Jungian Lens hosted on my own web site rather than hidden on an anonymous blogging site that separated me from my alter ego. I needed to come clean in the world, to be honest with myself and others. This need for transparency, to be authentic became something vital to the process of my healing post-Camino. I had my wife's support. I chose to begin looking at naturism as a form of alchemy. Psychological alchemy is a process that allows a person to deal with the trauma of the past, trauma that continues to hold a person as a hostage to the past. Bit by bit, the threads that bind one to past trauma are exorcised, burnt away. I shared this naturist and psychological approach to transformation change on both of my blog sites.

I began to reinvent myself, to transform my life through a blending of naturism, Jungian psychology, and Buddhist meditation. At the same time, our house was being renovated with new siding, windows and doors. It was synchronicity; two seemingly unrelated activities that mirrored each other. As I changed, so did our physical home. Our home, like all homes, was the symbol of our union as a couple. The Camino had taught both of us that as I had changed, we changed. As she changed, there became more room for me to do the next stage of transformational work, of healing my body, mind and soul. The interconnectedness between us, a conscious choice to remain together and work life out together demanded that we both become aware of each other and to risk the changes that were yet to come.

As I began this conscious approach to healing, I continued to practice meditation.

> *"As I meditate nude, there is a blossoming of energy that touches the roots of my body as well as my mind which embraces so much more that what I should know. And as I am awakened to this 'bindu,' I experience a freedom that far surpasses that of simply being clothes free. I feel the fullness of being a man, the fullness of being a child of the god and goddess of all creation."* [December 12, 2012]

Bindu is a term that describes the upwelling of energy in body, mind and spirit. Regardless of the word and its meaning, the important thing for me was the fact that I felt healthier, mentally and physically when I meditated nude. It was a moment of pure honesty, no cover-ups, no masks, nothing to hide behind and no need to hide.

The renovation work on our home in Saskatchewan was completed only days before it was time to leave for our winter stay in Latin America.

> *"In just a few hours I will be on a plane heading south to a warmer place. I have booked a studio suite in Puerto Morelos just a few steps away from the Caribbean Sea. Actually, the studio is located about two kilometres north of the town, a more secluded location, a quieter location. I wonder what changes will occur in me over these months away from my home in Canada. How will my relationship with M be transformed as I am transformed? This is a shared journey, not only a winter get-away, but to a continually changing future of our relationship."* [January 8, 2013]

We left Canada for Mexico and a small fishing village called Puerto Morelos. Our arrival into warmth and sunshine was a celebration, a return that was not under the same dark cloud that existed several years earlier.

We walked the beach to the town, a walk that took us alongside a nudist resort where couples were nude on the beach and in their lounge chairs. A bit further down the beach towards the town, before we reached the main beach we saw another couple laying naked beside the sea, sunbathing. This was unexpected, a shock to my mind which had always believed that nudity was a private activity, not a public activity. Somehow, the idea of sex got in the way; a belief that one only was naked in public as an exhibitionist. Yet, here we saw ordinary people, naked in full view, tanning as if there was nothing shameful about being nude in public. Shame existed only in the minds of those passing by who blushed at the nudity in front of their eyes. Shame was a state of mind, not a state of reality.

Even though that realisation came to me, I continued to hide my body while meditating nude. It was only when my wife pointed out some relatively private spots along the beach near the nudist resort where I could sunbathe, when I was finally able to take my nudity outside of the studio. I took her idea as permission to be nude outside of the privacy of our home. Realising that our relationship wasn't at risk, I gave myself permission. It was hard, for deep in the background there were echoes from the world of the Catholic Church that told me nudity was a sin. Being nude might not be a sin, but being nude so that others could see you definitely was a sin. Nudity was about sex, and that was that. I knew better, but that fundamentalist beast within told me otherwise. Yet, I dared to test creating a safe spot for sunbathing along that stretch of the Caribbean Sea. I sunbathed between the sea and private land guarded by a fence. I lay in the sunshine in a shallow basin beside bushes that would hide me from eyes of passing beach walkers.

My wife asked why I was a naturist in an attempt to figure out what was going on inside of me. Why did I need to be nude? Why did I need to be naked when the rest of the world, the civilised world was doing well with all of their clothing on? I attempted an answer on the Naturist Lens blog site.

> *"This morning, I opened up the door to the question during my time for meditation which then lasted longer than usual. It was essential to let the question stew for a while, allow the contents within to become stirred up in the darkness of the unconscious.*
>
> *As a child I was sexually abused, emotionally abused, physically abused in my family of origin by my biological parents. The sexual abuse extended to include my maternal grandfather and more than one parish priest.*
>
> *It was soon after the sexual abuse from my maternal grandfather, the last time I was sexually abused as a youth, I found myself in a quiet meadow in a nearby small forest with a book of poetry. It was a warm late spring day, about six months following this last incidence. Feeling the warmth of the sun and feeling the words of classical poetry, I soon found myself naked. Over the next two years, my last two years at home, I took every opportunity, weather permitting to hide in this forest and meadow in order to be free.*

Yet now, the pull to nudity is again strong so I look to these roots and it dawned on me that it is being nude where I claim control of my body, control of my identity, control of my sexuality. My body is not about pleasing others, making life easier for others. It comes down to control. Am I in control or do I defer control to someone else?

Now, in my sixties, I am saying this is my body and I will care for it, and my identity, and my psyche as best I can. I will not be a child and give control to another. I am a man, not a child victim continuing to seek approval, seeking to please others while disregarding myself." [January 25, 2013]

As the end of January approached, and with it the time to relocate to Belize, she showed me a perfect place for my nude meditation near our studio. She had thought that meditation at the end of a pier would let me meet the dawn, the time when I usually meditated, in a natural state. Though it would put me in full view of early morning passersby on the beach, I would be far enough away so that all that would be seen would be my back as I meditated facing the rising sun.

The next morning while I was meditating at the end of that pier for the first time, she took photos of me in meditation while facing the rising sun. One of those photos would become the cover of a book of poetry yet to be written.

We left Puerto Morelos, took a bus to Playa del Carmen, and then took another bus from there to Corozal, Belize.

Chapter Thirty-Four

Our ground floor apartment in Corozal, was beautiful and quite large. The garden outside the apartment, opened up to an abandoned field which made the garden area quite private. I knew that I wouldn't have to leave that garden in search of a quiet spot near the sea for sunbathing or dawn meditation. I had my own secret garden in which I would continue to do the work of healing skyclad. Wrapped in nothing but the air, the sky, I focused on breathing and releasing old pain.

There wasn't a beach for us to walk along each morning, so we were left to walk the roads and streets of the community. This was disappointing after our experience of walking ten kilometres along the beach in Puerto Morelos. We had committed to a month's stay in this small city so, we decided to accept what we were given in Corozal, and to learn what we could while there. It was pointless to complain when what we had was good.

I meditated, I sunbathed, I wrote blog posts, I read, we went walking to learn about the community and take photographs. There was no pressure on us to do more than this. I was relaxing, feeling the tensions of the past loosen. The journey to Corozal had begun to show me its purpose. I wrote in my Jungian Lens blog site:

> *"Another sunrise photo taken in Corozal, Belize, however this time the photo was taken by M while I was meditating in the garden ... au naturel a few feet away ... meditating in full view of passersby is something I would have never consciously done in the past. Always it was something to be done in an isolated situation, usually behind closed doors ... at home in my community.*
>
> *Few know that I meditate, none have seen me meditate, and perhaps even fewer would accept the notion of meditation skyclad. I have become aware of the shift of behaviour from shadow behaviour to conscious behaviour, purposeful rather than reactive. I now live as fully and honestly as I can."*
> [February 9, 2013]

Finally, with a sense of place firmly beneath us, we began to explore beyond the borders of the town. Exploration stopped being an act of escape, a way to flee from being too much together and reacting out of too-much-ness. We explored to learn and experience Belize beyond the borders of Corozal

Before our time in Corozal came to an end, we had decided that we wanted to return to Puerto Morelos and the long beach if it was possible, rather than to go on to the next place we had booked in Belize. We cancelled our next lodging in Belize and booked ten days in Playa del Carmen before returning to Puerto Morelos. The remaining days in Belize became even more relaxed knowing that we were returning to Puerto Morelos.

Playa del Carmen had very little to offer in the way of privacy which meant that nudity was limited to rare times on the roof top of the condo building and within the tiny two-room condo suite on the ground floor. Regardless, my mood remained positive as the beach was beautiful, perfect for our long beach daily walks. We had even discovered a tiny, private space at the southern edge of the beach where being nude wasn't an issue. That secluded corner allowed me to add to a growing collection of photos for a book of poetry that began to take shape in my mind. Ten days went by quickly. We left Playa with positive memories and returned to Puerto Morelos.

Our new home in Puerto Morelos was in the back section of a house called Casa Sorpresas. The house had belonged to an American woman who had retired to the town as an artist. She had died and her art studio had been listed as a rental by her daughter. This was the first year the studio had been offered for rent. The studio fit us perfectly, especially because of the sunny garden area surrounded by high walls. I again had my secret garden, my sacred space.

Living in the community of Puerto Morelos met all of our expectations and more. We had the best of living in town without losing the beach and the kilometres of sand for our daily two-hour walks.

Along with daily walks along the beach and more walks around the town, I spent more time writing in the garden. The privacy of our garden allowed me to write skyclad. My writing began to focus more and more on poetry than it did about writing blog posts. It was as if I was being transformed by the sun. I was being baptised as a bona fide writer in the process. It was the birthing of my writing skyclad, a birth that would lead to writing as the final element in the healing process. I was daring to tell my story, telling the whole, naked truth without holding back in order not to disturb or offend others. It was time for transparency and honesty. Then, my wife asked me why I find it necessary to tell the whole world rather than keep it private.

> *"I guess the best answer that I can give, is the answer I give her, that in keeping it all private, there is an oppressive sense that I am hiding in a closet in order to stay safe, something that I physically had to do as a young child. I hid in boxes, closets and elsewhere hoping to be safe. And as I got older, as a youth, I learned to hide within myself, build barriers so that I would not be seen and thus not hurt, as much. As an adult, the barriers were thick, so thick that I lost track of that which had been hidden and protected myself along with all the garbage, the history and the shame. I was a successful, very successful teacher, coach and therapist. Even though I am an introvert, I was able to be active enough in the community. It all worked until the barriers began crumbling.*
>
> *I am somewhat of a slow learner when it comes to dealing with change. I spent years trying to patch up the cracks with no success. When it finally became evident that I couldn't stop the collapse of the dam holding back all that I had denied about myself, denied to myself, to my wife, to my family and to the world, I ran – literally.*
>
> *In spite of the running, in spite of a return to meditation and becoming a Buddhist, in spite of a return to naturalism and of taking the opportunity to relax in retirement, I found that I continued to deny myself. I continue to look to others for permission."* [March 21, 2013]

It was time for me to stop asking permission, always trying to second guess what others wanted of me, trying to reshape myself to fit into those expectations. Telling my story, exposing everything, was all about setting the context of where I came from and how I survived extensive childhood trauma. I wrote in order to allow others to finally get to know who I really was. It was at this time that the Naturist Lens blog site shifted. I began to post images that were more personal, taking an even greater risk with being honest about who I was.

One of the risks I took without realising that it was a risk, was in taking my nude meditation into the garden area. As the weeks had gone by, the sense of privacy allowed me to feel invulnerable. This garden was my safe place. I still continued to go to sunbathe near the clothing optional beach, but meditation was saved for my secret garden.

With just a few weeks remaining in our stay at Casa Sorpresas, the woman who had rented us the studio walked into the garden while I was meditating. She saw me and silently retreated only to come back a short while later as my meditation was almost done with a gift to give to both of us, a deck of cards that featured her mother's art work. She ignored the fact that I had no clothes on. She then asked if we wanted to rent the studio again for the next winter. It was as if I had just passed a test. In spite of my nudity, she was willing to have us back as seasonal renters.

I began to write even more poetry, this time as part of a National Poetry Writing Month project at the beginning of April. I was writing purposefully, poetry that was naturist, poetry that would expose and honour my inner self, my authentic self.

> *Just Sit There – In Your Skin*
>
> *Reaching for the pillow, my seat,*
> *then reaching for a towel to cover*
> *pillow and the ground as cushion*
> *I walk out of the villa into the yard*
>
> *Facing the sun, I place the pillow just so*
> *carefully refolding the towel, placing it*
> *so it covers my seat, a naturist habit*
> *then folding the rest to cushion the ankles*
> *against the hardness of the patio's surface*

I take my seat and take a deep breath
signalling body and mind that it is
time to let go of everything but breath
Breathe in, breathe out, pause
Repeat and repeat until even the
concentration is gone and all
that remains is emptiness
a strange full emptiness
not nothingness

[April 2, 2013]

We had two weeks left in Puerto Morelos and we had already booked for two months at Casa Sorpresas for the following winter. We would have to find a place for January as the owner of the studio had already booked that month for someone else. For the remainder of our time in Puerto Morelos, we both relaxed with the knowledge that we were going to return to this same village and the same studio with my secret garden.

It was time to pack our bags and for me to put my clothing back on. Our home in Saskatchewan was waiting for us.

Chapter Thirty-Five

Life returned to some sort of normal back in Saskatchewan. It was a newer and shifting and constantly changing normal that had to take into account that the couple who had left in January had both changed and were continuing to change even more with the passing of time. In spite of the weather, my naturist tendencies remained with nude meditation, and braving the cool spring weather while being skyclad on the prairie hills on rare occasions.

> *"A few months ago I posted why I have shifted my life to include being nude at opportune times – at home, in private nature spaces and along clothing-optional stretches of beach. Nothing has changed since that post other than the sense that my need for being clothing free seems to be stronger than ever. Not only do I feel that naturism is part of my healing process, I also have begun to experience joy. Simply being without clothing brings a sense of lightness to my spirit. It is as though I have escaped from a locked box in which the universe is darker and sadder. Who wouldn't want to feel more joyful in their lives?"* [May 11, 2013]

So, now what I needed to do was to fit naturism into my life in Canada without offending others. I knew that I didn't live in a bubble. I lived in a real world that was either absolutely opposed to nudity, or simply quite wary of those who chose to be nude. People have been socially programmed to be fearful of nudists, afraid of their intentions. I had no intention of having my nudity break our family bonds or our friendship bonds. I didn't know with whom my being nude would be the factor that would bring an end to a relationship. And through all of this testing of boundaries, my wife was on edge. She feared that I would cross a line that would then impact on her community and family relationships. Tension crept back into our lives.

What remained the same was our commitment to our family and our community friends as we began the regular round of visiting and being visited in return. We travelled to North Dakota to take part in the lives of our grandchildren there before returning home to host my brother and his wife as they travelled making their own connections to extended family. Then it was off to the north to visit our son who had relocated to work in the Oil Sands projects in Alberta.

Near the end of May, we went to visit a few people who were part of the Prairie Suns Naturist club near North Battleford. It was a small event with just three others including the host couple. We spent an afternoon in the sunshine with our hosts and left after a potluck supper. We had made new friends, but I didn't know how we could maintain this friendship and have it become part of our larger life because of nudity. It was okay for me to be nude in the isolation of their acreage. However, it would not be okay to have them return to our home and be nude there.

I found myself disclosing more and more of my life history on the Naturist Lens blog site, old stuff and new realisations. I began to understand more of what I could only call, naturist spiritualism. Synchronicity lead me to find a web site by Ed Raby Sr, called "All Things Rabyd." The author of the site was a Protestant pastor who wrote on various spiritual and religious themes.

Tucked into a part of his web site was a number of articles that discussed the topic, "God and Nudity." There were quite a number of articles that investigated the spiritual value of nakedness. The articles spoke of the holiness of being "Naked before God." Pastor Raby talked about nakedness in both physical and spiritual terms and showed how the two blended together. As I read, I began to let go of the Catholic idea that nudity was sin. By approaching naturism as a spiritual practice, I began to give up the idea that being naked was a perversion. Being skyclad was okay and perhaps, even a holy way of being present.

As my allergies had continued to be a problem for me, I had decided to continue the series of allergy treatments I had started in Toronto, with a centre in Estevan, a five hour drive from our home. Because of its close proximity to Green Haven Sun Club, I made a decision, to go to the naturist site following treatments rather than make the return five hour trip home the same day. The treatments left me quite tired, too tired to safely drive.

So began a new chapter in my life as a naturist, the world of sharing my naturism with other naturists. In early June I went to Green Haven for the first time. In my journal, I wrote:

"So far, it is quiet with only a few people tucked into their trailers because of the coolness of the weather. In spite of the coolness, I am reluctant to go back into my trailer because of the sunshine even though it is weak and not "warming." It is the thought that counts. With the prediction of cloudy and rainy weather for the next few days, this is it.

I have learned something from Buddhism, be present in the moment and not focused on the past or the future. The present has sunshine and a brisk breeze and I am outside, naked. Life is good." [June 13, 2013]

The journal continues explaining:

"Nudity is too important to me at this time to risk having it sabotage my healing. Nudity is a major aspect of my healing journey, a way of washing away the sins of the past committed upon me and committed by me. Feeling the heat of the sun almost cook me is best described as being in an alchemist's cauldron being changed and transformed and purified. I will go into that more at another time. It is enough now, to say that as I lay in the sunshine, totally present with the rays and the heat and in my body, I feel a healing stirring within me. In a way, it felt as though I was being washed and cleansed, being purified by light. As I said before, this all has the feel of a spiritual journey." [June 13]

This first visit to Green Haven had taught me a lot about being whole as I lived without clothing for a few days in spite of cool weather. During that time I found the courage to dig deep within myself and confront various fears that continued to linger close to the surface. I read, I wrote, and I breathed deeply. I knew that I would return to Green Haven, alone again if I had too. I needed this freedom to be without clothing, rather than not return out of fear about what others would say about me.

Where was all this nudity taking me? And, how was it affecting my wife? I was caught somewhere between being authentically myself and living an increasingly artificial life with my family and community. I could sense the tenseness each time I was nude at home. Boundaries became the issue. Where and when could I be nude was constantly being negotiated and re-negotiated, usually on a non-verbal level. Each time I cut back too much on being nude, I would get very agitated and there would be a corresponding response to that agitation by my wife. When I was too much nude, she got agitated and again we would find ourselves reacting, setting off each other's triggers that activated our complexes. It was a very uncomfortable dance.

Near the end of June, I returned again, to Green Haven. Going alone meant that I got to be nude as many hours as I chose within the campgrounds and my wife was insulated from having to deal with my constant nudity. Returning to Green Haven alone was an attempt to give both of us what we needed, a solution that hopefully met both of our needs for that moment in time.

> *"Exactly what is the other reason for being here? Is it to write a book? Is it to discover some level of peace within myself? Or, is it more about returning to life, to a restoration of presence in life? Perhaps it is all of these things. I do have to admit that for the most part, I am simply here and not all that actively here. M is quick to note that I have no passion, no drive and that I have a hard time to initiate any kind of idea or activity. I leave it all up to her. And, she tells the truth of it. I guess I could best describe my presence as my body is here but mind my is on extended leave of absence leaving my ego holding onto the shell of who I was, who I could be. My guitar sits untouched for the most part though I can sense the echo of an old passion to play, to sing. When M sends me off to do what I need to do to get healed, I wonder if this naturism process is part of the solution or simply a diversion in keeping me at a safe distance from what I need to deal with."* [June 25, 2013]

I didn't really know the answers to the questions popping up in my head. My intuition told me one thing, and my ego told me the opposite. I had taken a book with me to Green Haven, by Robert Moore, the author of <u>Soulmates</u> and <u>Care of the Soul</u>, two books I read in the distant past. The new book was called, <u>Dark Nights of the Soul</u>. In it, I found something that helped point to a possible answer to my dilemma:

> *"Many people think that the point in life is to solve their problems and be happy. But happiness is a fleeting sensation, and you never get rid of your problems. Your purpose in life may to become more who you are and more engaged with the people and the life around you, to really life your life. That may sound obvious, yet many people spend their time avoiding life. They are afraid to let it flow through them, and so their vitality gets channeled into ambitions, addictions, and preoccupations that don't give them anything worth having. A dark night may appear, paradoxically, as a way to return to living. It pares life down to its essentials and helps you get a new start."*[20]

"A return to living," that had to be the best way to describe what had been happening to me, over and over again. I slipped into depressions where I would be confronted by ghosts and shadows of the past. I waged war, defeating these monsters over and over again with each descent into the dark nights of soul. And then, I would be reborn, resurrected as a changed person with each return to active living once free of the spell of depression.

In early July, a message that was sent to me by my son challenged me to look at the idea of happiness being a fleeting sensation.

> *"Over the past couple years or so you've spent a lot of time soul searching and dealing with your demons. You've mentioned I believe that before that life kept you busy and you pushed them aside in a sense to take care of and raise our family. From there, you traveled and did many other things to try and hide from them.*

---

[20] Moore, Dark Nights of the Soul, pp xiv-xv

Now, to me anyways, it appears you have been focusing directly on the demons and facing them head on. A step that likely needed to be done. But how long does this phase last, and when do you go back to finding hobbies, enjoying day to day life without having to put all your energy into healing? I understand and respect your efforts of using various tools like meditation, Buddhism, Jung, and nudism to heal and feel whole, but if that's all you make your life, your final years will be just that, with small clips of other stuff tossed in.

At some point I think you'll need to move past this and start fully living in the outside world again.

Does the level you seem to attach and immerse yourself into these various coping mechanisms perhaps detach you from reality and the outside world, making you feel better/safer on the inside, but also denying you the real world experience?"
[July 5, 2013]

Was Buddhism about detachment? In a small way, it was about detachment; however not a detachment from life, but a detachment from the negative thinking in order to be mindfully present in my life. After meditation I found that I had more ability to attend to the people around me, a better ability to participate in activity. Without taking time for meditation I found it very difficult to leave grip of the shadows and the ghosts that haunted me.

Was Jungian psychology about detachment? For me, Jungian psychology was about making myself aware of what was going on beneath the surface of my brain so that I could move out of helplessness. With more awareness of how I was triggered and what lay behind the triggers that sabotaged my behaviour and beliefs about myself and others, I became more rational and present. It became more about separation rather than detachment.

Nudism? With the experiences of the months prior to receiving this message, I had learned that there was no detachment at all in terms of my ego in relation to others. What did exist was a separation of my life into places and times for nudity, keeping that separateness from others who would be disturbed by my nudity.

My son's letter had me evaluate what I had been doing so that I could move forward with awareness and not get lost in substitutions for living a real life.

Chapter Thirty-Six

"The capacity to love, in the face of the absurdity of our ends, permits us to live an enlarged life."[21]

On my third trip to Green Haven, I wasn't alone. In relationships that hope to last, it is vital to find a way to try and understand the other person in the relationship. With understanding, choices become based on reason rather than being reactions out of fear.

> *"While walking this morning, M was talking about those she has met and the others whom she has heard about from the lady who takes care of registrations. She noted that it appears that almost everyone appears to be wounded in some way, making Green Haven more of a naturist retreat centre than a naturist club. Since I referred to my initial visits here as engaging in a naturist retreat of one person, her idea made a lot of sense. It also fits in with my book project that looks at having naturism become a therapy model for healing, depth psychology work."* [July 10, 2013]

For the next few days, we shared my need for naturism and nudity, including interactions with others who were also nude. We didn't talk about what to do or not do, we just became fully present in that small nudist community, and fully present to each other and those with whom we met.

After five full days at Green Haven, it was time to return to everyday life. Following our stay at Green Haven, we went on a two week tour for visiting extended family, distant friends, and hiking. For those two weeks depression and shadows became distant memories, for the work I had done using all the tools I had at hand, had allowed me to be present, to be positive, and to enjoy the days away from home. I had continued to write in the quiet moments I found along the way, but I didn't feel anxious when those moments didn't appear with any regularity. Then we returned home.

---

[21] Hollis, Creating a Life, p. 126

"Today is not such a good day in the grand scheme of things for me. Every once in a while I crash and find myself having to pick up the pieces and put them back together again like some senior citizen Humpty Dumpty. After two weeks of putting myself out there in a fairly active manner, I simply had run out of energy. That is one of the problems of being an introvert." [July 30, 2013]

I needed time to withdraw and recharge my internal battery. This need wasn't about my being wounded, but more about my being an introvert. We had three days at home to recharge our energy levels before some of our grandchildren and their parents arrived to spend some quality time with us for summer fun. Three days had been enough time for me to again be fully present enough to play with my grandchildren during their visit. When they left, it was time for me to return to Estevan for more allergy treatments and another stay at Green Haven. For the second time, I didn't go alone. With our first shared time at Green Haven being so positive, I was surprised when on the second day of this second stay, conflict erupted, a conflict that was focused my need for nudity.

"M is talking about endings again, about how we are too different and that we need to follow our separate paths. She can't change anymore to fit into how I am changing. If we are to survive as a couple, there is no room for naturism and I need to become less of a loner, I need to fit better into community making it easier for her in the community. I need to like clothing like she does so that there is real attraction as there is no sexual attraction when there is only nakedness. As all this spilled out with tears, I sat quite, stunned. I didn't react with off the wall anger or self-critical comments. I let her words sit there, heavy. I am too taken aback to process this information in terms of what next." [August 14, 2013]

Before the summer was over, I made one more trip to Green Haven, alone. I retreated from being nude in front of my wife at home in hopes of making it better for both of us. I hated conflict between us. I didn't want to risk our marriage because of my need to be nude. My head was swirling with the fear that I would somehow slip up and put our marriage at risk. Nudity was kept hidden behind the door of my home office where I wrote and meditated.

As autumn approached, we began to talk more and more of walking the Camino together. We decided to spend a number of days in Saskatoon hiking the Meewasin Trails to test our bodies, and to see what we needed in terms of training and equipment. We set our sights for walking the Camino for the fall of 2015. We wanted to be prepared physically and mentally for that challenge.

Summer had left me feeling better physically than I had felt for years. The allergies had retreated. As I looked back over the summer I found that my attention to meditation and to naturism, with an active program of allergy treatments, had been a good part of why it had been the best summer I had experienced for many years. And then I realised that the work in Calgary with analysis, and the walk through a part of France on the Camino had also been significant contributing factors to my improved mental and physical health. Was I healed? No, there was no fixing the past. I simply had been able to cope better. Perhaps the writing and the poetry had also contributed.

I had begun to write poetry again in the fall of 2013, naturist poetry that I had begun writing while in Mexico. I had the intention of publishing a book of my naturist poetry. Writing was therapy for me, as much as meditation and naturism was therapeutic. In the Jungian Lens blog site I wrote:

> "*I take photographs and I write. These two things have likely done more for my finding and maintaining a decent level of mental health. Both photography and writing bring balance to my life. I don't write to figure things out, I write and things straighten themselves out below my level of conscious awareness.*" [September 27, 2013]

Writing had become a focal point of my day, as much as my meditation. Both were done while I was nude most of the time. I wrote for my blog sites, I wrote poetry, and I wrote simply to write. I didn't know it at the time, but I was apprenticing for a larger task, the work that would become this series of books. I began to put the poetry I had written, into book format.

"My focus is to finish my poetry book. I am having a trusted colleague read the poems with a critical eye while I struggle with gathering the photos for this collection of poetry. Why images? Well, it is just how it is with me. When it comes to depth, to soul, to the spirit, I find a compulsion to bring in images in order to access the depths. It is as though images open doors that take me out of the mundane world and into a rich and fertile, inner world. Like writing, photos have become part of the therapy process. They are more than simply photos of being naked. They show hidden truths about who I am." [September 29, 2013]

The book was published as <u>Naked Poetry: By the Sea and on the Prairies</u>. I then turned my attention towards the writing of a novel for the National Novel Writing Month project, hoping that I could write a 50,000 word novel in thirty days during the month of November. With the poetry book completed, I began to write a practice novel to see if I had it in me to write consistently at the required pace. As I wrote, it became difficult to separate truth from fiction. It seemed no matter what I wrote, a part of me seemed to slip into the writing.

"So, what is the "real" story of our lives? Are they all real or all unreal, all provisional? There are the stories we tell ourselves, and the stories we tell others. Some of them may even be true. But what are the stories which are storying their way through our daily lives and of which we are mostly if not wholly unaware? What are the stories that represent our rationalizations, our defenses, the stories in which we remain stuck like flies in molasses?" [22]

Reading this in part of a book sent to me by James Hollis, a Jungian analyst and author, I decided to base the novel I was going to write on the story of how I came to meet my wife. It would be a fictional only in terms of the names of characters and the dialogue between characters. The plot would tell the real story. I had never written about any of this part of my life in the past. I had firmly believed that there was no need, that this was too private. Even when it came to

---

[22] Hollis, Hauntings, p. 5

writing as therapy, journaling as therapy I had avoided telling this story. However, everything had changed within me. I intended to have fun with the story.

The novel, On The Broken Road, was finished in less than a month. It was to eventually become the second book in the series in spite of the fact that it was the first one written. This is the third and final book in that series.

Then I began the process of editing the novel, listening to both my inner critic and to the voice of my wife who had highlighted those areas which made her feel uncomfortable. I listened and doubted myself, even berated myself for having spoken in the novel in ways that seemed to cause more harm than good. I was ready to burn the book as I had burnt so much of my writings in the past. The resulting storm between us passed as it had always passed in the past. I took her ideas and reworked the book. Scenes were deleted, conversation was stripped of offensive language, and what remained was approached with more care in retelling the tale. In the end, the novel became more than ten thousand words longer.

I sent all of my siblings and my children e-book versions of the books I had written, the naturist poetry book and the novel. Both books had been also published and available for sale with a print on demand service. Now, all I had to do was wait for the royalties to pour in. As expected, my children were quick to tell me that they liked the novel. What was unexpected was the response from some of my brothers and sisters. Those that wrote to me were very supportive, pleased to have been included in the novel as characters, and I was even more surprised that what I said in the novel had matched what they saw as the truth about our family.

The novel showed the darkness, and the primary role of nudity in escaping that darkness during a period of time that spanned just one year of my life. As I wrote, the pieces in my head began to be pulled into a sort of order. I then knew what I needed to do with the story of my first twenty years of life that had been journaled over and over again as bits and pieces were remembered. I would have to write that book next, the first book of the Healing Skyclad series.

Chapter Thirty-Seven

"... each person in a relationship brings to it ... complexes,
which are active and forever ... always there, silently gliding
through the back rooms of our souls ... we understand why
harmonious relationships are nearly impossible."[23]

With the novel <u>On The Broken Road</u> completed, I found it difficult
to return again to reading, meditation, and to outer life. So much had
been activated within me with the writing of the novel. I was again
depressed and sensitive. An underlying depression that I began to
suspect had more to do with seasonal darkness than it did with
pressing shadows, had settled in. Rather than write about my first
twenty years of life, I wanted to write the follow-up story to the
novel, tracing our life together from where the novel left off.
However, the words refused to be written.

I retreated and waited.

"I am again writing poetry. I have written seven poems so
far. The poems are arising out of my re-reading When Things
Fall Apart: Heart Advice for Difficult Times, by Pema
Chodron.

Fear is Natural

The door is there, within reach
Beyond the door an unknown
Or is the unknown on this side
Within the body that stands
At the door peering out into the darkness
[December 20, 2013]

By Christmas 2013, life became better with family and friends
giving of themselves to make our lives together all about love in
various forms and states. There were no thoughts of naturism,
Jungian psychology, or Buddhism. However, just before the New

---

[23] Hollis, Creating a Life, p. 134

Year I found myself writing a lengthy blog post at Jungian Lens about my nudism. It was a post my wife said I needed to share. It was important to her that others understood why I was behaving so differently, why I felt compelled to write so much about naturism on my blog site.

> "This is a hard piece of writing to bring out of my mind so that you can read it and perhaps understand a bit more of who I am and why I am the way I am ... I am a stranger to myself as much as I am to everyone else; and in a way, that has been a deliberate strategy I have used throughout my life as a way to protect myself and hopefully protect those around me from the dark, dank and dangerous stuff that lies buried deep within me ... The past haunts me. Traumatic events leave a permanent mark on those who are traumatized. The trauma is coded into both the body and the psyche, that inner, intangible part of self ... PTSD – post traumatic stress disorder.

> Trauma has a way of working its way out of its imprisonment [within the psyche]. All it takes are triggers. ... I am damaged goods. I have become a conscious naturist and Buddhist as part of my healing journey. This is who I am and I accept it ... I can't change my past. I can't undo the damage I have done on my journey to get to today. But, I can understand and accept and find compassion for myself and others". [December 29, 2013]

The response to the post by both family and friends told me that the risking of disclosing my early history was worth the angst and the fear of being vulnerable. With that blog post, and with the novel made available to the public, I began to learn more from siblings and cousins about my family of origin, things that I never even suspected. And, I began to dread what yet would be revealed to me. I had opened locked doors and stuff was pouring out from all sorts of directions. More than anything else, these messages confirmed within me that I was not creating false memories. Others saw what I saw, sometimes they remembered seeing more.

I then began to write the sequel that would tell the story of the hero and heroine going on with their life together with the intention of calling that story, <u>Soul Magic</u>. Again, I had retreated from telling the story of the first twenty years, a story that needed to be told. I found myself running away, hiding from the work that I needed to do.

And then it was time to fly off to Mexico.

Chapter Thirty-Eight

"In any relationship a man is largely at the mercy of what he does not know about himself. And the extent to which is in the dark is the degree to which his own inner woman is projected onto another person ... a man is always falling in love with, or fearing, his own unconscious material."[24]

We arrived in Playa del Carmen and settled into our apartment in Casa Verde. Life in Playa became a place of sunshine and warmth, taking the place of the fierce cold we left behind in Canada. Since we had been in Playa del Carmen the year before for ten days, we quickly found a routine that took advantage of that knowledge as we roamed the beaches, and along Fifth Avenue. We walked until we were too tired to walk any more. Fatigue was the antidote to thinking and feeling too much.

Unlike, our first time in Playa where I had the rooftop patio as well as the tiny condo, in Casa Verde there was only room in the apartment for nude meditation and writing at the table, while nude. I felt frustrated with so little time or place for being out of my clothes. Even the south end of the beach, which had been a good spot for sunbathing the year before, was now off limits as it was constantly patrolled by police on the lookout for drug smugglers. It felt as if I was purposely denied the opportunity to be nude. And, as a result, I was getting more and more sensitive to the smallest things around me.

The ghosts exposed days before our departure from Canada had left both of us ultra-sensitive. The oppressive feelings that I had felt with the loss of time to be nude, had set me more on edge. A week after our arrival, a storm between us resulted in me taking down the Naturist Lens blog site for the second time. I blamed her. Then, out of guilt for having unfairly blamed her, I turned my anger and frustration onto myself, blaming myself for being so obsessed with nudity.

---

[24] Hollis, Under Saturn's Shadow, p. 42

Many of my naturist photos and my on-going journal were also deleted along with the Naturist Lens blog site. I sank into a deeper depression. It was as if by destroying all of it, I would be burning out whatever it was in me that caused us both so much pain. I was lashing out at myself for being so different, a difference that got in the way of my being the husband I needed to be so that we could remain married and happy together. James Hollis, Jungian analyst and author had it right, I was afraid of what was bubbling inside of me, afraid of that stuff which had been projected onto my wife. More than anything, I was afraid that I was going to find myself in a life without her.

It seemed to me that there wasn't room anymore for me to be different. If we were to survive as a couple, I had to become someone different, someone who was normal. With these self-defeating thoughts laying waste to my confidence, I gave up meditation completely and made sure that I wrote only when wearing shorts. My complexes had been triggered which in turn triggered my wife's complexes. It appeared as if there was no way we could survive the ongoing storms. We were just too different.

It took a few days after that explosion, for me to return to some sort of sanity. I took time to read more of Carl Jung's psychology, before that sanity returned.

> *"The shoe that fits one person pinches another; there is no universal recipe for living. Each of us carries his own life-form within him – an irrational form which no other can outbid."*[25]

I was pinching, trying to fit into a way of being that didn't fit anymore. I couldn't simply adopt my wife's reality as mine, nor could she adopt my reality as hers. As the heat settled, we became more careful with each other and around each other. The problem was that neither of us was being authentic or honest with ourselves or with each other. We both became victims of trying too hard to fit into the other. We were both walking on eggshells hoping to avoid triggering yet another storm.

---

[25] Jung, The Practice of Psychotherapy, CW XVI, par 81

"Like anyone else, I wanted to be in full control of myself and hated it when I wasn't in control, when it felt like others had control over me. Not realising that this lack of control usually had its roots within myself, I was quick to lay blame on others for stealing control from me. [January 19, 2014]

Control issues were at the heart of the silent conflicts, and that control conflict was centred on the issue of change for both of us. A changing sense of identity was at the centre. It looked and felt like the other partner had become a stranger. What was left was a feeling of having lost the person we had married and loved over the years.

Too much effort had been given to contain the past, to disguise it and hide that past. I had hidden and denied critical parts of myself, those things that had almost destroyed me and those things that nourished me because of fear. I was ruled by the fear of losing my wife if I fully revealed the man beneath the surface. The person beneath the surface was a stranger, not the man she knew and defined as me.

I didn't know this, consciously – no one ever does. The more one truly believes that they are one hundred percent how they appear and live, the more they are a victim of the denied parts of themselves. Between us, the control issue was now focused on my nudity, my struggling with trying to bend my need for nudity around her need for normalcy.

I had closed down the Naturist Lens blog site thinking that this would somehow make it easier to abandon that topic as a focus in my life. Yet, three weeks into the New Year, the inner pull drew me back into nudity, at least on an intellectual level. It appeared on my Jungian Lens blog site. It began with a return to reading Pastor Raby's blog posts in "Nude Before God." As the pull was an act of the unconscious, the shadow within me made its appearance first in that return through poetry.

"Standing Naked Before God

Sewing fig leaves without needle or thread
Desperate to hide shameful nakedness

What was good is now evil
Being made in the image
And ashamed of being in that image."
[January 21, 2014]

I captured myself twisting and turning in the posts at Through a Jungian Lens. It didn't matter that I had shut down the Naturist Lens site, the exposure of myself through words continued, the wrestling with self-identity was highlighted. I convinced myself that I was simply examining an interesting blog site from a psychological point of view.

The sequel to the novel <u>On The Broken Road,</u> was abandoned just as I had abandoned the Naturist Lens blog site. I knew that I wasn't ready to tell that story, nor was my wife ready for it to be told. That story could not be said until I had the story of the first twenty years re-written and given out for others to read. I had to settle my debt with the ghosts of those first twenty years of my life.

Just before the end of January, another storm saw me cutting up the swimming briefs that I had bought in Thailand two winters before. I was crumbling and becoming more and more irrational due to self-denial more than anything else. I had been too busy trying to erase the man I was becoming. I wanted to be an acceptable man, even more than acceptable as a person. What I was doing wasn't working.

My wife had recognised that I was again going backwards, slipping into a depression with my attempts at disowning nudity. With her encouragement, I regained enough balance to replace the swimming briefs before we left Playa del Carmen for Puerto Morelos.

I looked forward to returning to Casa Sorpresas. I had talked with the owner about my being nude in the walled yard. She didn't express any problems with my being nude and gave me permission to continue being nude in the garden for meditation, writing, and sunbathing.

In comparison with the previous year, there were no naturist photos taken the winter of 2014 in Puerto Morelos that were not destroyed with the exception of one that I had used for a Jungian Lens blog post, a photo that had been taken by my wife. I had been determined to disown the fact that I needed so much nudity. In my mind I believed that I had to escape the compulsion of nudity so that everything would then be better between us. My nudity became tightly controlled and confined to safe and private moments, indoors for the most part, with the exception of early morning meditation and sunbathing when there was virtually no chance of being seen by anyone.

The first week in Puerto Morelos was hot. I went sunbathing by the sea in secluded sand dunes. We went walking along the beach for hours and then went for a swim in the sea. Even writing was set aside for the most part as I readjusted to living again in Puerto Morelos. It was time for both of us to let the sun and the privacy of our little garden even out the rough edges that had been exposed while we had been in Playa del Carmen. And then I slipped into another bout of depression.

> *"I am quieter than normal and a good part of that quietness is due to being caught in the swirling waters of depression, denying the depression and as a result, causing myself and my life partner too much grief in the process. It is hard to see 'self' in any kind of good light when depression re-enters the picture."* [February 11, 2014]

Two years earlier I had been in Thailand ready to return to Canada and Jungian analysis because of depression that grew out of too many flashbacks of childhood abuse. I now needed to tell that story of abuse, and so I began to write. Without thinking about it, I began slipping into being nude more often. It seemed as though nudity was as much a part of my writing, as was the keyboard of my computer. Nudity was part of the letting go of the dark images that emerged as I wrote about the first twenty years of my life.

The story consumed me as I wrote and exposed new memories. I found backup material hidden in old file folders that had been hidden and unconsciously protected from my irrational moments of 'burn and destroy' when I tried to erase the fact of being in this world. Thankfully, the hard and painful writing of my old journals gave me a solid base for the retelling of my early years of life.

I had decided that I couldn't turn the story into a novel though I did keep the names of the characters fictitious that I had used in <u>On The Broken Road</u>. I wrote the truth, as I knew it while growing up. I wasn't simply making it all up. If I was to make the book public, others such as my brothers and sisters, who knew a good part of the story, deserved to hear the truth. The story was to be presented with all the fictional names of those in the story, I had to protect the innocent and the guilty, and perhaps more importantly, I had to protect myself.

> *"It wasn't long ago that I believed that it was important to keep the peace, even if that meant not speaking about something that needed to be said ... This avoidance of exposing ghosts and setting them free only allowed those phantoms of the mind and memory to dominate the inner spaces of myself, ensuring that inner peace would never become a reality ... And so, I now find myself too tired to play this game. I haven't done anyone any justice in keeping a smile on my face and keeping the peace ... Now it's time for me to stop hiding, stop disguising, and stop trying so hard to please by twisting myself like a pretzel into shapes that would please others. It's time to risk being vulnerable and being patient, about accepting without judgment the fact of who I am and how I am in this world."* [February 20, 2014]

Our Saskatchewan neighbours arrived in Mexico to spend four weeks in Puerto Morelos, in lodgings not too far from ours. The separation of our residences allowed me enough privacy time for nude meditation and writing while nude. Our neighbours were well aware of my tendency towards nudity. Both had seen me nude in the past. They knew me as a person and they accepted this naturist side of who I was.

Soon enough, the time in Mexico came to an end and we returned home.

Chapter Thirty-Nine

"The self is relatedness; the self doesn't exist without relationship. ... You can never come to yourself by building a meditation hut on top of Mount Everest; you will only be visited by your own ghosts ... you are all alone with yourself ... The self appears in your deeds, and deeds always mean relationship."[26]

While in Mexico, during the last month of our winter getaway, I had begun to relax again in our little casa. In spite of brief storms, my being nude seemed to have become less and less of a problem. In my mind, I began to think that my wife had finally become more comfortable with my nudity. But, once we were at home, her discomfort reappeared. We were at home and not in Mexico. In Mexico, we were safely anonymous. At home, that wasn't the same story. At home, nudity had to be kept behind closed doors and drapes. Nudity, my nudity, had again become a problem. Boundaries needed to be re-established. However, my need for nudity didn't so easily disappear, it simply went into hiding, only to re-emerge in the hours when I was alone at home. When I was alone the boundaries were no longer needed.

Then, our focus turned to the Camino which we had planned for 2015. It was time to focus our energies on developing confidence in being able to walk a distance of twenty kilometres a day while carrying a backpack. As well as our focus on the Camino, I continued to write poetry using the National Poetry Writing Month as motivation. And, I continued to work on my story. I had written quite a few poems in Playa del Carmen and Puerto Morelos, perhaps enough for the second book of poetry. But, I wanted more so that there would be choice when it was time to gather the poems together for the book. My naturist wanderings in the prairie hills had provided me with new material for the poetry collection. And these stolen moments of naturism revived a will within me to explore further, what made me well.

---

[26] Jung, Nietzsche's Zarathustra, p. 795

After an absence of three months, I revived the Naturist Lens blog site which had been stripped of many of the photos I had taken and used.

> *"I have been gone from this site for almost as long as I was in Mexico. In fact, I thought that the site had completely disappeared. It was a message from my host server reminding me to update the WordPress software that I used that made me realise that this place was still in existence though it wasn't visible to the world. A few clicks and the renaming of a file soon had this site re-appear so that I could talk again with you. Is this a good thing or not?"* [April 11, 2014]

I believed it was a good thing though I was uncertain enough of my wife's reaction to my recovering and restoring the blog site. I kept silent about the revival of the blog site, in spite of the fact that she had once encouraged it. She had protested its destruction. She had even suggested that I provide a link to the naturist blog site on my Jungian Lens site. I stayed silent about its revival for I didn't know if it would survive long. The element of trust had been weakened within me; I didn't really trust myself with its continued survival. I didn't want another slash and destroy mission to upset her as it had the last time. I wasn't willing to risk disturbing the peace between us that had emerged as we did all the normal things of life together. I kept my writing, my meditation, my time nude in a separate, safe, and in my solitary world.

All of my energies all focused on writing when time allowed between our hikes and visits to and from family and friends. Near the end of April, I again began to take naturist photos. It was as if I was beginning to thaw out as the first of pleasant spring weather began to make an appearance. I felt my whole being open up as though I had just been released from solitary confinement. I became happier in spite of a return of allergies.

> *"When I am alone, I do almost everything wearing nothing but my birthday suit. The only concessions I make are for weather and safety. Sometimes there are tasks that require*

protection of the body. To try to do everything nude is not an intelligent decision." [May 12, 2014]

With the warmer days of late spring and early summer, I returned to the prairie hills and being skyclad. It was as though nature was my cathedral, where I entered into a spiritual world. The darkness was banished in my head and heart during these holy moments in nature while skyclad. It also became easier for us to be with each other, finding enjoyment in being together as my depression disappeared.

The poetry project had been completed with the edited poetry being returned to me from a trusted friend, who was an author and a university professor. All that remained were the photos to be chosen to accompany the poems. It was too difficult to match up the poems with the photos that were left in my archives. In an attempt to solve the problem of naturist photos, I invited naturist friends from social media, to participate in this second book of poetry. I was able to give them a poem so that they could take a photo that would best fit their understanding of the poem. It became a social naturist activity fully based on cyberspace interactions. A few other photos were taken by me that would include both me and my wife. The work of getting the book ready to publish was left for a later date.

The Camino took over most of the time that remained. We both read of Camino adventures of other people, we hiked at every opportunity when weather allowed, and we tested out our hiking gear. I began to believe that we were actually going to do this, walk the Camino. I was beginning to believe that we would be ready to handle the daily uncertainties of where to sleep and the prolonged stress of walking twenty kilometres every day for more than a month.

"Today I was able to get out for a walk in the warm sunshine without having to wear clothing. I only had to drive about seven kilometres where I parked the car on a rarely used dirt road. From that point on, there were no farm houses or highways to intrude on my privacy. It was an incredible feeling having the sunshine warm me to the very core of my being while I walked another two kilometres on the faint trail. I have claimed this small part of the universe as my retreat centre." [May 17, 2014]

Only my allergies were a problem that just didn't seem to go away with summer approaching. I found that I needed to return for allergy treatments. I had hoped to make retreat stops at Green Haven with each scheduled appointment, but somehow life got in the way. I felt the loss of naturist time at Green Haven keenly. I had been prepared to spend time at Green Haven without my wife, as I was certain that she would refuse to go with me. Weather was the main reason for my having to cancel the stays at the naturist club near Regina. My wife saw how I slipped back each time my plans had to be cancelled. She then suggested that we could visit a different naturist venue later in the summer. It surprised me that she spoke of going to Helios, the naturist campground near Edmonton, and it lifted my spirits. Thinking, maybe I was wrong about her response to social naturism, I was filled me with new hope. But again, life and weather got in the way. I began to feel that the universe had deliberately put naturism in last place.

Summer was family time with our children and our grandchildren. Camping adventures were added so that we could hike long nature trails that would give us a better experience with hills and wild trails.

Because of the weather and my giving her the space she needed to be free of my nudity, we became more relaxed with each other. The tension eased. There appeared to be an expansion of tolerance which gave me more space for being nude. That feeling of a new normal seemed to be becoming more acceptable to others as well. It was early July when an event confirmed my sense that my being nude in my home was okay.

> *"I was sitting in my usual chair, reading, while M sat nearby, talking on the phone, when one of our friends who had visited us in Puerto Morelos, quietly entered our house. Usually when this neighbour entered our home, she called out as she knew that I was often nude. She has seen me naked numerous times, something that was probably more of a shock to me than it was to her.*

> *She entered our living room where I sat while reading nude, in my Lazy Boy chair. She sat in the rocking chair next to my*

chair and handed me a piece of paper. She asked me to write out the rules of a card game she intended to play with her grandchildren while camping. Taking the paper completely exposed me. The fact that I was nude made no difference to her. It was as if being nude was normal and acceptable. I was surprised.

M told me that the rules were in the cabinet in the dining room. I hesitated. It would mean that I had to stand up to go and get the rules from the cabinet drawer. I thought about how it would look to see my genitals swaying back and forth while walking to the cabinet and back, Sensing my discomfort, M went to the games cabinet calling for our friend to go with her. With the rules written out, she left with a thank you. I guess we now have a new "normal" in our home." [July 7, 2014]

Nothing was said following this event about what had happened and life went on as normal. Camping, hiking, studying about the Camino, visiting, being visited, reading, and writing were the summer rituals that marked my life. On rare occasions, conflict would arise and then subside without threatening our relationship. It seemed that we were both moving on with life, accepting the changes that had appeared.

However, as the weeks passed, the more I relaxed within what I thought was the new normal, the more there was an increase in tension within my wife. In the last half of August, another storm erupted. Limits regarding my nudity at home had again been reached and breeched. The storm left me again fearing for the survival of our marriage. I didn't have a plan for a life without her, or for what I had to do if it all came to an end. As I listened to her pain, I heard that there was no hope for us, that our differences were too great. And then she asked a question, not for the first time, of what I needed in terms of being nude. She deserved an honest answer. From my journal, the words I sent in response to her question:

"What do I need when it comes to being free from clothing? I guess the best answer is simple, whatever I can get. I know that when we are at other homes that the opportunity for going without clothing is limited to sleeping and taking a

shower or bath. When we walk the Camino, I know that there will be little opportunity for being nude. I accept all these limitations just as I accept the fact that I can't walk down the streets of our town or walk the grid roads nude.

But at home? I need more than sleeping and bathing. Being nude is like a gift that is about being free to be all that I am. I don't have to hide behind clothes or roles or social demands from me. I need all that I can get to balance out all the other times and situations where there is nothing to get. Being nude not only feels good, it lifts my spirits, puts a smile on my face and heart, and in my opinion, plays a large part in my healing.

What would be best? Knowing your limits so that my nudity at home doesn't cause "us" problems. Our togetherness comes first above everything else.

Now, what would I like at home? No boundaries in the house other than what is necessary for your well-being. I would like to be trusted to stay within proper boundaries such as down rarely used paths far from people with the knowledge that I am always alert and ready to put on what is needed when it is needed. I would like to be able to go as a couple to various gatherings where others will be nude. Of course, what I like and what will be possible won't match up as I do have to consider your limits, your boundaries.

I am not sure if this helps or not, but it is a start." [August 20, 2014]

For the rest of the month, I existed at the edges of depression, more sad than happy. With an active increase in camping which let us engage in long and longer hikes, the sadness receded. The story being written of my life as a child was drawing to an end. How much my sadness had to do with the story, was likely significant. Over the summer, new information had emerged from contact with two of my sisters, cousins, and other members of my extended family. I took what I learned and made corrections.

Finally, on October 7th, I gave my wife the last chapter to proofread. The book had been written. My son was also reading this final version in order to find errors that need to be addressed before I got the book published. A Broken Boy on a Broken Road, was published on October 22nd, as an e-book, and I gave it away like the other books.

With the arrival of November, I again found myself participating in the National Novel Writing Month. I was intending on writing a true novel. I was done with writing my autobiography. I needed to step into a different world, one that left darkness and embraced light. With all of the study and planning that had already gone into preparing for the Camino, I set the novel on the Camino. Thirty days of intensive writing was the plan with the hope that I would write at least fifty thousand words in the process.

As with all things one writes, the novel captured a lot of what I had become, as the main characters of the story were drawn out of the world of naturism, Buddhism, and Jungian psychology. The Camino trail itself that was presented in the story, was the real Camino path with real towns, cafés, hostels, churches, and geographical features.

> *"I have been writing a novel that focuses predominantly with the depth of spirituality that one can access while nude. History has taught us so much about being clothes free when approaching whatever it is that is the source of our soul, our spiritual centre. It is only in relatively modern times with the dominance of the three desert religions that nudity has become the portal to evil rather than the portal to the temple of heaven within each of us."* [November 27, 2014]

I completed the novel, A Small Company of Pilgrims, and turned to finish up the second book of poetry. I had managed to get quite a few photo contributions for the poetry and was left with only a few final photos to add before publishing the book. Finally, just before Christmas 2014, the second book of poetry, Naked Poetry 2: At Home and in Nature, was published.

Feeling a high level of confidence, the plans for book three in the poetry series was made. The focus would be on Jungian psychology using images of the masculine, the feminine, and the union of both into a holy marriage. I had three books that I planned on taking with me to Mexico which would guide me in the process; <u>He</u>, <u>She</u>, and <u>We</u>, books by Robert A. Johnson.

Chapter Forty

"There is real vulnerability for both therapist and the person entering into this work of depth psychology. It is as though the establishment of temenos, a safe and sacred space, that one becomes safe enough to strip off their psychic layers as if stripping off clothing in order to expose the wounds that had led to the therapist's office." [November 2012]

As I wrote during the autumn and early winter, I had forgotten what the motive was behind my being engaged in naturism. Nudity did its healing work behind the scenes. By the end of 2014, it seemed as if naturism itself had become the objective rather than it being a healing process. I simply wanted to be nude, I enjoyed being nude. I had come a long way from the crash in late 2011 that had sent me back into Jungian analysis. I was better than I had been for more than ten years. Naturism had become a vital part of that return to a better level of mental health. Believing that I was 'fixed,' I thought that naturism needed a new reason for being in my life.

Naturism then became a crusade rather than a sacred, spiritual part of helping myself to heal. And with a new poetry book planned, the roots for the idea of the naturist poetry book was questioned. I began to think that I should focus on Jungian concepts rather than on naturism as healing. I couldn't see how I could justify the journey into inner and outer relationships with nude photography. I was at a loss as to how I would proceed when it came to photographs from a Jungian point of view. The poetry was straight forward, as it would be based on mythology. Yet, if it was to be book three in the series, nudity was needed for the photos that would accompany the poems.

My ego had swollen with so many people now reading the stories of my childhood and youth, as well as the two books of poetry. I celebrated thousands of downloads of my free e-books. In my head I had finally arrived on scene as a writer of note. But, the shadows within knew a different story of who I was. Within, deep beneath the level of my awareness, I was still a scared and vulnerable boy; a boy who had turned to being nude in nature in order to begin the long, long process of healing my soul.

Christmas with family came and went, and then it was time to leave again for Mexico. I was in greedy anticipation of the warmth and sunshine. Though I didn't admit it, even to myself, I was yearning even more for the chance to be out of my clothes. There was feeling of safety and comfort in the familiar little studio suite in Casa Sorpresas, in Puerto Morelos. I had again contacted our landlady to make sure that I still had the freedom to be nude. The last thing I wanted to do was assume and get us in an indelicate situation. I didn't want to risk having to find some other place to live. To be able to meditate outdoors without clothing allowed my spirits to lift out of the confines of a cold winter where being buried under layers of clothing was essential.

As we settled in to our studio suite in Casa Sorpresas, I began the task of re-writing a story I had written in 1979 about my wife's father. The original version was a stapled booklet that needed to be edited and expanded upon in order to be worth reading for the younger generations of her family. The first three weeks were spent alternating between the family book and cleaning up the final version of the pilgrim novel.

While I meditated and wrote, my wife took a number of photos of me, something she hadn't done since our last time in the studio. She then asked about my photo plans for the poetry book. She had noticed that I wasn't fully immersed in rewriting the story of her father. It was obvious that I was agitated with not working on the poetry that I had told her would be my primary project. She approached the topic in talking about the photos for the She part of the book. I then realised that she was ready to be the photo model for the section on the feminine psyche, and the section on the holy marriage, the We section. She was doing her best to lighten my mood which was fraying.

As we talked about the poetry plan, it felt to me as if the poetry book had become a shared project. She had suggested that we take the photos based on my overall plan, so that I could write the poems with the image as a visual reference. I would brainstorm photos scenarios before heading out to take photos. She let me know when her limits had been reached with nudity. We would then pause the photo shoots while I wrote poetry using the photos already taken.

She was fully involved in either being in the photos or taking the photos for the complete project. We began with photos in the garden before venturing off to locations along the sea and in the sea.

> *"You'd think life would get easier as one gets older. As I am learning, if anything, it gets more and more complicated each day. It seems that just as I learn yet one more answer, a dozen more questions leap into existence to challenge my right to say I am becoming wiser as I get older. At this rate, by the time I am seventy-five I will effectively be a dunce. What a difference from my youth when I believed myself to be smarter than parents and everyone else that I knew at that time. Not only I believed that to be the truth, but so did all that knew me. And then began the painful process of growing up and growing with awareness that every single truth that I knew was a fiction."* [February 14, 2015

Over the period of a month all the photos were taken to fit the planned sequence of photos for the project. After every photo shoot we would go over the photos with my wife making the final selection of which photos I would use. With her final choices made after each shoot, I would then write the poems to fit those chosen photos. When the project finally came to an end, I felt that we had done something beautiful together, that somehow nudity had stopped being an issue dividing us. I came to believe that we had entered a new phase of relationship where nudity was beautiful.

> *"Every truth you held close is questioned, and often exposed as a self-deceit. You have to strip away all preconceived notions in order to see clearly the self that lies hidden in the shadows of the swampland, a self that waits for ego to allow it to emerge into the light of day as a newborn emerges from the birth canal – naked and untainted in spite of the long period of gestation in a dark, damp place."* [February 16, 2015

I had come to believe that 'we' had arrived in this new future in perfect harmony, to a place where there were no more demons, no more shadows lurking in the darkness. But that was far from the truth. She had the courage to tell me that in spite of the poetry project, she was not a naturist. She had simply acted out of a belief that I had needed the project to succeed for my own mental well-being. She clearly stated that she had taken the last nude photo and would not have any more nude photos of her taken. In spite of her statements, the afterglow of the poetry project left me hopeful of better times to come, better times including more shared naturism.

The rest of our time in Mexico became a time for simply being together. For me the time, sunshine, meditation, naturism, trusting in the process had become the healing balm that worked to banish shadows and ghosts. I was coming to understand more about the power of naturism as vital to my well-being and began to think that I needed to share this path that had finally allowed me to regain a stronger sense of self, self-control, and balance. The idea of nudity as therapy which I had first thought about in the summer of 2013, returned.

> *"The idea of shedding clothing as a part of a therapy practice in a private, safe space has nothing to do with self-gratification, it has nothing to do with sex. In the setting of your sacred space, removing your clothing is a visible note to oneself to be honest, not to hide. There is the key aspect that I have discovered, that of taking the psyche to a time of innocence and trust. For self-therapy to be effective, one must risk and trust that the risks taken will heal and not harm the "self."* [March 23, 2015]

Chapter Forty-One

"In place of being at the beach to honour the appearance of the sun each morning, I am able to be in our garden fully nude. Typically I time my meditation so that the first rays of sunshine to enter the garden area will touch me, illuminate me. It becomes a very spiritual time for me. It is as though I am having my body filled with light and warm that comes out of an inner peace. M and our landlady who owns the house in which we occupy her deceased mother's art studio, both honour this time as they quietly do their things, sometimes passing by me in the process. I would have never thought that this would have been possible three years ago when I first "intentionally" adopted naturism as a mode of therapy.

In the past I have talked about experiences using nudity as therapy, including references to literature on that topic. I sense that it is about time that I returned to this theme for future posts here. I am hoping that rather than having a focus on the nudity that can too easily become fixated upon displays of genitals, the use of judicious editing of images will convey honest nudity in a manner that allows the words to be heard. I don't want the images to get in the way, but I do think that images are vital in the process, a means of having the walk and the talk become one." [March 7, 2015]

Before we returned home to Canada, I had begun to organise for our fall adventure, the Camino de Santiago. The planning was needed. A benefit that grew out of the planning was that it turned my focus away from being present and placing it somewhere into the future. We were both anxious to get back on track with training and making this shared dream happen. I was able to return to the present because of my books which were being published. The free e-books had been removed from the host site which had informed me that nudity was against their policy. As a result, I entered the world of commercial publishing.

With the two books about my life now published and available in print form, I ordered enough copies to give away to my family. I also ordered copies of my three books of poetry.

The books challenged me in ways that I hadn't expected. It was one thing to have the books as e-books floating around somewhere in cyberspace, but with them now in my hands, I was left with the question of what to do with the physical reality of these books.

I had no answers at that time, only the realisation that I had to find answers. Putting my life and my secrets onto paper and into books had been a protest. The time for hiding and silence was over. The silence had been broken, I had hidden myself in fear and shame. In hiding I began to try and heal myself while failing miserably. With the help of others, of mediation, and the honesty of naturism, I was finally able to accept that I could be okay even though the trauma of my childhood and youth would likely continue to give me grief. The books I was writing were vital to learning to forgive myself, to let go of debilitating shame. There were no more secrets.

Not long after our return home to Canada I got the news that the brother closest to me in age was in the hospital. My brother had fallen grievously ill and wasn't expected to live much longer. I managed to get to the hospital in Edmonton before he passed away. Though we had fought as brothers always did, we had a bond forged by shared survival in a home filled with abuse. We had gone separate paths and rarely communicated once we left that home. Standing at the side of his hospital bed with only the pressure of his hand squeezing mine in response to my presence, that distance was erased. Nothing could change the truth that we had shared too much to ever be less than brothers.

> *"As each of us descends into our personal darkness, we lose hope, self-respect, and time to share with those who care about us. [I didn't have a chance to say good-bye to him. With this brother, I got that chance."* [April 18, 2015]

The fallout from his death caused me a lot of grief as I wrestled with things that needed to be done: gathering documents, notifying agencies, and trying as best I could to bring some sort of order out of the chaos of his life so that his children could understand this man who had been so broken in his childhood, too broken to have been the father that they needed him to be.

As I struggled with these things, I remembered the good and the bad times and realised that it could have been me dying leaving chaos behind me and hurting my children in the process.

Life then slipped into a quieter place for a while for me once I finished doing what I could for my brother's family. My wife returned to working at the nursing home while I tried to sort out the past from the present which had come up with my brother's death. Without deliberately planning it, I again went into the hills for silence and healing as I had in the past when the pressures began to overwhelm me. Meditation and sunshine, walking and sunshine became my rituals of healing.

And, as always when she was at work, I lived without clothing. When she was at home, I found the boundaries for being nude had been stretched so that I could meditate in a secluded but sunny corner of the yard, and sunbathe on the deck with the railing blanketed so that any passersby in the back lane wouldn't be unduly surprised in seeing a naked man. I would write in a corner of the deck, while I had a covering ready should it be needed.

In early June, my wife agreed to go with me for the second time to take part in a Prairie Suns naturist event, a pot-luck barbeque. Our hosts were glad to see us again. Because we hadn't attended the previous year, they were unsure that we would attend. The day was warm and sunny for early June, making it easy to shed clothing. We played several games of Bunnock, visited with other couples, and enjoyed the food. I sold my three poetry books to our hosts before we left with a promise to return again.

At the end of June, she went with me to Green Haven. Again warm weather and good company made the days spent there pleasant. We had visited others, we had taken walks, we read, we sunbathed, we swam in the pool, and we spent our private time free of clothing, without a storm appearing on the horizon.

Life had changed. All the evidence before me told me that my nudity had stopped being an issue.

My books finally arrived by parcel delivery from the United States. What did I want to happen with these books?' I needed to be honest in answering this question. It couldn't be that I hoped to make money selling them. My community and friends needed to know the truth of who I was, and perhaps understand why I was the way I was. So, I put the books on sale in the community of Elrose, my home community, and in Lanigan, the community where I had raised my family. I then put a copy of the two volumes of my story in the local library.

Offering the books for sale wasn't about making money. I knew I would never sell enough books to make a living at writing. Yet if I sold books, it would require me to account for the money earned. The idea of giving profits to the Sheldon Kennedy Child Advocacy Centre which focused on helping people dealing with sexual abuse was adopted. I wanted my story to make a difference.

For my community, my motive was about being authentic in a way that invited the world I knew to know the truth of the man they had known as principal, teacher, neighbour, friend, or in whatever role they had known me. Getting the books out there was a different sort of nakedness, a risk that worried me. Would these books cause the people in my community to distance themselves from me? Would neighbours and friends keep their distance because I dared share my stories, my photos, and my poetry that revealed what perhaps should have been left hidden? Where had my life journey just taken me?

> "*Embarking on a spiritual journey is like getting into a very small boat and setting out on the ocean to search for unknown lands. . . . but sooner or later we will also encounter fear. For all we know, when we get to the horizon, we are going to drop off the edge of the world.*"[27]

---

[27] Chodron, When Things Fall Apart, p. 1

Yes, I was feeling that I was approaching the edge of the world, that in exposing myself, naked physically and psychologically, I was going to fall off the edge. However, my fear had no basis in reality. No one had abandoned me. My honesty had opened doors that I had never realised were closed. My presence in community was based on my roles in the community. Now, I had become an ordinary person like them, a damaged man who was more than a bit afraid.

> *"It is a simple, patent fact that when a man discloses his self, his inner experience to another, fully, spontaneously, and honestly, then the mystery that he was decreases enormously."*[28]

Walking and training, travelling to see grandchildren and their parents, interacting more often with extended family following my brother's death, a return to a Prairie Suns Naturist event, some naturist time together at Green Haven Sun Club, and the preparations for the Camino had all pulled me back into being present in life. Scattered though all of these activities were many moments of healing naturism.

Yet, it wasn't all sunshine. My blog sites became silent. Attempts to write fell flat, and too often I retreated into silence. Something was still pushing from the depths and I pushed back. I didn't want anything more to mess up what I had rescued and claimed as my life. Besides, I had a Camino to walk.

> *The strangest thing that I learn as I age is that time spent clothing free is vital to my well-being. Too many days without conscious time spent nude and my spirit gets very agitated. It's as though I find myself going through a period of withdrawal. Yet as soon as I get to meditate au naturel, or be blessed with being bathed with the sun's rays, I find myself in peace and at one with what I can only call "spirit." It almost feels as though I have entered a form of religious ecstasy. Could it be that naturism filled the spiritual vacuum that came with a loss of religious faith?"* [July 11, 2015]

---

[28] Jourard, The Transparent Self, p. 3

I had been often seen nude by our neighbour who had spent time with us in Mexico. She didn't hesitate to go into my office where I wrote while nude simply to say hello before heading back to the living room to have coffee and a chat with my wife. There was no need to rush to cover up after being seen nude so often. Trust had been established so that I didn't have to worry about her taking my nudity into the community as gossip.

On occasion, I was also seen nude by another neighbour, while I was on the back deck. Typically, I reacted with covering myself up while on the back deck when I realised that she was there, usually after she called out to say hello. It had happened with some regularity. I covered up so I wouldn't be seen as flashing, as an exhibitionist.

> *"This afternoon our neighbour said "Hi," as she passed by the fence through which I was barely visible while sitting at a table writing while skyclad. She then came into the yard while I sat writing on my laptop. She approached me to ask if she could have some beets from our garden. There was no comment about my nudity. I hadn't expected her to enter the yard after the greeting so I hadn't covered myself. Getting an affirmative response, she then went into the garden to pick the beets then returned saying thanks as she then left our yard. It seemed as if it was okay to be me, even a naturist me."*

She had bought all of my books not long after I had received them, and had read them all. It shouldn't have surprised me that she would accept my nudity without any critical comments about it. But, I did wonder if the fact that I was often nude would somehow negatively affect her friendship with my wife.

With the Camino only weeks away and with our training having taught me that we were ready to make the eight hundred kilometre pilgrimage, I began to see the Camino as more than a physical challenge than a journey of healing. For me, it was becoming another face of spiritualism.

I wasn't going to walk the Camino for religious reasons, so why was I walking? It wasn't enough for me to say that it was simply an adventure on my bucket list. My life seemed to be turning towards a more spiritual focus that appeared in the books I read, and was heightened by meditation and naturism. The Camino was going to be a testing ground to see if I would find myself worthy. I would have to find answers somewhere between Saint Jean Pied de Port and Santiago.

Chapter Forty-Two

We left Canada on August 23, 2015 and arrived in Paris the next morning with the plan of taking an overnight train to Bayonne in the south of France where we would take a different train to our destination of Saint Jean Pied de Port. While we were in Paris we decided to walk around the Left Bank in order to pass the long hours between our arrival and the late overnight train to the south of France. We were too hyped to sit still very long. Before we returned to the train station in the late afternoon, it rained. We arrived at the train station soaked and tired.

> *"Someone asked me if I was going to walk part of my Camino skyclad. To be honest I don't think I will even try as there are hundreds of walkers in front of me and behind me, usually within sight, being passed or passing us in turn. The journey has a different impulse, a different goal, something that I can only suggest touches on the spiritual dimension. All pilgrimages work a change on the psyche and spirit of the men and women who walk them, a change that is not very predictable, sometimes not even wanted as it disturbs the way we live in the world and understand the world."*

When we got to Saint Jean just after the lunch hour, we registered for the Camino and bought our scallop shells to put on our backpacks, the symbol that would identify us as pilgrims. We were tired from all of the travelling we had done in the past two days, however we decided to go exploring in spite of that fatigue. We both knew that we couldn't have gone to sleep anyway. There was too much to see before we took our first steps on the Camino the next morning. We roamed through the picturesque town, found something to eat, took a lot of photos, and finally began to slow down.

We began our walk the next morning on my wife's sixty-fifth birthday, with a short day of walking to Orisson where we had booked ahead of time. At Orisson we made our first connection with other pilgrims, some of whom we would meet again and again until we arrived at Santiago. We celebrated my wife's birthday with thirty-five people singing "Happy Birthday" to her. We had begun our Camino well.

The second day, we walked considerably longer and we arrived in Espinal, Spain, by mid-afternoon. Between the long hike and the heat, we were very tired. On the third day, we walked twenty-four kilometres with a rest stop in Zubiri en route to Larrasoana. It was our forty-fourth anniversary:

> *"Here on the Camino we walk within ourselves, our hands holding onto walking poles that click off the kilometres. It's hard work, tiring work. At the end of six hours of walking we are dead tired and want nothing but to shower and perhaps take a rest before we set out to discover the small community we have chosen for our night's stay. This late afternoon walk is done hand-in-hand just like the walks we take around our home town. With no poles to occupy our hands, it is as though magnets force our hands to seek each other. The mind doesn't play a role in this phenomenon – magic is all that can be said to explain it. I admit it, she is my Magical Other."* [August 28, 2015]

Over the next several days, we walked in very hot conditions which left us exhausted and willing to relax when opportunities arose. We walked through Pamplona rather than stay in the city. We were reluctant to stop when a village lay only a bit further, a more suitable kind of stop for us. On the fourth day, we left the main trail to visit an old Templar church at Eunate. It was the first church we had entered since beginning the Camino. In the church I found myself thinking of the violence, the betrayals, and the power of the Templars. The ghosts that assaulted me in Conques, France three years earlier, were absent.

> *"As we walk we are both finding long moments when we are simply aware of the path, the air, the horizon, and our bodies. Thinking has faded, that noisy chatter that typically obsesses our attention. During moments like these you are fully aware of the world around you and the people near you. Yet you are walking a singular journey, your own 'Camino of one.' And this is the way it is supposed to be, even when you walk with a partner."* [September 1, 2015

We continued the Camino walking longer distances as we felt very strong, at times walking more than thirty kilometres. As had become a habit for us, we stopped only when hungry or when our socks needed changing, and then pushing on. It was as if we were obsessed with not wasting time while getting to where we were going. The idea of simply being present began to slip away to be replaced with targets of distance and hostels. Of course, when that happens, there is always a price to pay.

We entered the Meseta, the drier agricultural plateau, once we passed the city of Burgos. We had finished the first third of the Camino, the testing of the body, a test that we both seemed to have passed without injury, not counting the constant aches and pains that came with walking long distances every day. The second third was about testing our minds, our will to complete the work of walking the Camino.

On the second day out of Burgos, I began to limp because of a growing blister.

> *Pain arrived as my blisters decided to be heard over the silence of the prairie. But I wasn't concerned at all about pain. The vista that spread out before us was too interesting to be missed. So, as we have always told our children, I sucked it up and found a good measure of peace in the process. We walked on and reached a ruin of an old 15th century church and pilgrim hospital called San Antonio. I was caught by the use of both the Tau cross and the Templar cross that advertise the fact that a small part of the ruins is still being used as a pilgrim refuge. The hospitalero working there was an older Canadian who took time to tell me a number of interesting bits of information about the history of the place."* [September 9, 2015]

I took the usual precautions and treated the blister twice en route so that I could continue walking. By the end of that day, when we were in Castrojeriz, the blister had infected and became a blood blister. There was no way to continue walking until I dealt with it. I became depressed with the reality that I would have to take a bus back to Burgos, undoing the last two days of walking, in order to be seen and treated by a doctor. I was told that I wouldn't be able to continue walking the Camino for at least a week.

Staying the night in Burgos, at the same municipal hostel we stayed in when we first arrived in the city, we tried making the best of what appeared to be a bad situation. The idea was that my wife would continue to walk while I took buses. We would meet up each day to stay together in hostels until I could walk again.

The next morning while having the dressing changed with a positive response by my body to the treatment, I got my wife to take photos of the materials that were used to treat the blister. I was determined to continue walking the Camino the very next day, even if it meant only walking ten kilometres. As soon as we left the hospital, we found a drugstore where we bought the needed dressing materials and antibiotic cream. Then we went in search of a pair of hiking sandals that would leave the blister and dressing untouched by any strap. I left my hiking boots in the hostel. Feeling much better, we took a bus back to Castrojeriz where we met up with a couple that had become our best friends on the Camino.

I walked twenty kilometres the next day. I had paid my price for pushing too much in the heat and now it was time to be fully in the Camino listening closely to my body and not focused on deadlines and destinations.

> *"The path diverged today at Poblacion. One way followed another canal to Villalcazár; the other followed making a minor highway, on a senda – a fine gravelled path that is considered to be the main path. I chose this route in order to be kinder to my foot, after all, I was still supposed to be in Burgos getting my dressing changed this morning. But, I chose to follow my heart and listen to my body. And that, is something we must all do."* [September 13, 2015]

Two days later, it was my wife's turn to be physically tested. She started to limp because of foot pain. We stopped in Sahagun soon after it began to rain, a good thing as she needed to give her foot a rest. I had been battling an upset stomach which had drained me during the walk that had left me feeling a more than a bit woozy. It was very hard to concentrate on the hiking as my stomach roiled. I had a hard time focusing on the path ahead of me. I had walked in front of my wife, not really noticing that she was beginning to lag behind me.

When we finally reached Leon, we had arrived at the end of the Meseta, the second part of the Camino. We got there in mid-morning, in time to buy some hiking sandals for my wife, hoping they would make a difference for her foot which had become more of a problem. With the new footwear on, we then kept on walking, stopping for the night at Villadangos. Feeling encouraged by a reduction in her pain using the new sandals, she wanted us to push on to reach Astorga the next day, a thirty kilometre walk. It was her turn to not listen well to her body and the pain returned with a vengeance.

We walked each day, fortified by our resolve and by frequent doses of ibuprofen to deaden the aches and pains. We reached the Cruz de Fero, the iron cross at which we had intended to leave stones we had carried with us from Canada. However, seeing tour buses and hordes of pilgrim tourists surrounding the iron cross, we decided to walk on past the tall Cruz de Fero to find a quiet rest spot.

> *"A bit further down the trail we found a bench where we could savour the silence and take time to think about our family and why we were walking. We had walked more than 500 kilometres to get this far, suffering and rejoicing at the same time. As we sat there, a small number of pilgrims passed us, all lost in their own thoughts of their own pilgrimages."* [September 21, 2015]

The Camino then took on a new face, as we entered Galacia, the last province on our pilgrimage.

"We left Fonfría at 7:30 this morning with the ambitious plan to walk long, very long. After about a hour, the view of hills and valleys was given a magical appearance as low lying clouds flowed over the hills like white water waterfalls. Add in the colours of dawn and the spirit soars. We almost forgot about sore feet." [September 27, 2015]

The walk from Fonfria ended up being much too long, more than thirty kilometres, as we risked trying to make it a stop just before Sarria. The cost in terms of pain and the aggravation of her injuries made us both wonder if we would be able to walk the last hundred and seventeen kilometres into Santiago. The next day was the hardest day we had endured since we began the Camino. We were thankful to find a bed in Morgade after walking only seventeen kilometres. It looked as though our Camino had come to an end.

The next day, we began to walk tentatively, ready to have someone call a taxi for us, or at least for our backpacks if the walking got too tough. We walked slowly and gently. The easing of our pace and the lessening of our expectations allowed us to keep going. And with that, our spirits picked up. We walked about twelve kilometres to Portomarin where we stopped for the rest of the day and the night.

"It was another magical day of moon, mist, old oaks, and ancient artifacts of men. As we came down the small mountain we found ourselves entering into the mist. It was a place where there were no shadows, only possibilities. It was a time and place for letting go of certainties, a time and place to accept what is, rather than what the ego says should be." [September 29, 2015]

As we walked the last few days of the Camino, the crowds of pilgrims got larger and noisier. Pilgrims without backpacks passed us by as if we were standing still. They were in a rush to get to the next stop where often a bus would be waiting for them. I was getting angrier and angrier at these pilgrims who hadn't taken the long route, the path through suffering and pain over hundreds of kilometres, carrying everything needed on their backs. My anger shocked me. I was the one with a problem, not them. I wanted to control their Camino experience rather than focus on my own journey.

"Things get in the way of what we want to have, what we want to happen, or what we want to do. What gets in the way? For the most part our wanting, our beliefs and our expectations are at issue. In other words, we become the problem, only we rarely are aware of that. There is a condition many suffer called, "me, me, me," that is at the core of our collective dis-ease.

When this condition is present, one sees the world through a filter which has the self at the centre as if one is the sun and everything and everyone else was in orbit around the self. When too many as hyper self-centered, we have an angry, nasty, uncaring world. So just how does this belong here?"
[October 3, 2015]

The last two days of our Camino were walked in the rain. We were soaked to the skin, through our rain gear. We laughed in the rain as we passed pilgrims huddled under bridges. We walked along the trail which had been turned into a winding creek. We stopped from time to time to have coffee and meals. With the deluge giving way to a gentle shower, we walked the final kilometres through the city of Santiago towards the Cathedral and the pilgrim office in order to get our completion certificates.

It took us forty days to walk to Santiago. We both arrived suffering injuries from our long walk. Our original plans had been to continue on to walk to Finisterre and then on to Muxia. We had originaly planned to travel to Portugal and explore that country once our Camino had finished. But our bodies told us that we needed to stop and rest. My mind told me that I needed to stop and process what we had done.

Chapter Forty-Three

We caught a train to the south-east of Spain to the Costa del Sol where we could stay at a naturist resort in Estepona. With walking getting more difficult, we needed someplace quiet to sit still. For the next two weeks, there was no need to do any touring, any wandering around towns in order to take photos. We simply sat still taking advantage of the hot Jacuzzi and a cold swimming pool followed by soaking up sunshine, or simply relaxing in the quiet condo we had rented.

The two weeks in Estepona gave me time to sort through what had happened on the Camino. Unlike the attempt three years earlier in France, this had become a real Camino for two, a couple. We had learned to adapt to each other's injuries, pace needs, fatigue, and moods along the way, a mirror of sorts of the life journey we had taken as a couple over forty-four years. The two weeks also gave me time to release tensions that had to do with not having taken any time for meditation or naturism. Being in a naturist site, there was freedom for me to be skyclad.

We flew home to Canada at the end of October. And, as other times when we had spent time away from home, we entered into a whirlwind of travel in order to catch up with our family. I had also begun to write a version of what I had hoped would be this book. However, that all came crashing down. I stopped writing almost as soon as I had begun. I wasn't yet ready to write this story. I had thought that by having fictional characters standing in for me, it would be so much easier. But it was a total disaster.

All of my efforts at trying to be an authentic person, to unearth and uncover the truth of who I was just couldn't be buried under pseudonyms in a novel setting. The last poetry book had taught me too much about being transparent, about being honest. So I retreated into writing silence, preferring to invest in life with people and with myself. I retreated into sacred moments where I could be transparent, wrinkles and all.

And then, emerging out of the cold of winter and depression, I finally found the voice that I needed, in order to write this book.

"Behind the scenes I am shifting my writing into a new venture, that of a book that looks at nude psychotherapy. I consciously use nude therapy for my own self-directed therapy. Over the past decade I consciously tried to explain why I seemed to heal when the process was done while I was naked." [December 6, 2015]

I wrote furiously for ten days and then stopped. The need to be present at home was too vital. I needed to be with family. I knew that a return to Mexico would allow me the time to thaw and allow this story to flow unimpeded.

It didn't take long once we had settled back into our studio at Casa Sorpresas, for the words to begin flowing. As I wrote, there was very little room for taking time out to write any blog posts. However, there was time for making sure I wasn't absent in my marriage.

I finished writing the first draft in mid-February. All during the writing process, I continued to send my wife what I had written hoping that she would spot inconsistencies and missing pieces. I hadn't thought that in reading what I had written, she would respond emotionally. There were tears as old wounds were reopened by the reading. Yet, the words needed to be written and read for both of us.

And then, I rewrote that first draft, hoping to cut away the needless pain those words evoked. I approached the story with a more gentle touch. I didn't want to lose vital scenes, nor did I want those scenes to lay blame on others. Somewhere along the way another ten thousand words crept into the story. But, it was too personal in its inclusiveness of others. I needed to give others a distance so as to protect their identity and integrity. I needed to write the story again.

This final version is the third telling of the tale in a period of three months.

Chapter Forty-Four

> *"We cannot change our culture and its impact on us. And we certainly cannot change our personal history with the huge influence of parents, living and dead, or how we internalized that history and our cultural context, adapted ourselves to it in order to survive. Almost all of us, then, lost our way along the road."*[29]

This, the story outlining my life as a husband, father, and grandfather has been written. What remains is the work of making sense of what I have written and how I have changed as a result. "Am I healed?" becomes the dominant question that I face. "Are the ghosts of the past now at rest?" This second question perhaps is the one that is central to finding the answer for the first question. So, I will begin with this second question.

As Hollis explains, we really can't change what had happened to us in the past. It has taken me years of therapy, decades of writing, and a lifetime of hiding to finally realise this truth. Life happened. I was traumatized. I survived and buried that trauma and lived as though there had never been anything out of the ordinary in my life. I built a life that didn't have any place in it for my history, a life that was centred on others. I liked being undamaged, being competent, being loved and liked in the life I had created. I was certain that I was being honest with my world – what you see of me is who I am. I couldn't change the world, so I had changed myself. I lost myself in the process. It was as simple as that.

It was the biggest betrayal of all, the betrayal of myself. Midlife changed the rules. It became time to pay the price for putting my soul in solitary confinement. Midlife crisis gave me a choice, go on a journey of healing, or call it quits. This book tells the story of my choice and my journey. Like all journeys, I needed guides along the way, and I found them. I needed to remain responsible for my commitments to others while on the journey rather than abandon them.

---

[29] Hollis, Under Saturn's Shadow, p. 125

I couldn't change the world, but I had to return from my journey of healing to help others who were also on journeys. How had I managed to get from so wounded as to be incapable of being a husband, father, and teacher, to the place I am today. Somehow, in spite of a history I can't change, I have managed to remain as a husband, father, and now grandfather who is loved.

So how did this come about? With mental-health therapy, with taking quiet, introvert time-outs to allow me to have the energy to be more present with others, with mindful meditation to help quieten a mind that would race away on itself, with naturism and nudity to allow a sense of wholeness and complete control, with stubbornness to resist believing the inner voices that would have me give up, and with a stubborn clinging to love. It wasn't one path to survival and wellness. It was the full-meal deal, a recipe that was inclusive of all facets of myself.

I am in a good place now. I breathe easier and I have hope that I will finish this journey of life with my wits intact. I want these last years to be honest years, honest with myself so that I can be honest with others. I know that as I go forward into these last years, I will continue to hold close to me the people and the strategies that have allowed me arrive in my senior years in one piece – meditation, naturism, psychology, care of my body, and love. It can't be an either-or set of choices as I have tried leaving parts out only to crash over and over again. I will still fall flat on my face, but at least I now know that I will get back up and recapture an authentic smile with a real will to live and love.

This story is finished, but life goes on. Beginnings and endings are only important for books. I will continue to write until there is no call to write anymore.

Afterword

Naturism is a vital part of my life. It has taken me years to finally come to realise that it has served a vital role in bringing me back to life as a full participant. I had understood earlier that Buddhist meditation and Jungian psychology had significant roles to play in my healing, but the rawness of naturism was something that challenged me and everyone else around me. I have finally learned to honour everything that allows me to be fully present in life.

My use of naturism is not intended to cause offence. It is not about others or their opinions. Naturism is only about my relationship to myself. Thankfully, those closest to me have learned that truth and have accepted it. They have seen how naturism has allowed me back into their lives in a meaningful way.

Abuse, such as I had suffered as a child and while growing into a young adult, can never be erased. The post traumatic affects will be there for the rest of my life. If I had suffered a biological disease such as diabetes, no one would think twice about a need to take insulin for the rest of my life. Mental health issues that arise out of abuse are no different. One finds the strategies that work, and one uses those strategies in order to live a full life. If not, life becomes a living hell until death eases the pain.

I don't recommend naturism for others, but I don't rule it out either. Each person is different. We all have different needs, different wounds, and different broken roads to follow in order to become healthier humans.

Acknowledgments

No story can come into existence without the direct and indirect influences of others. It is with the guidance of Marvin Haave and Doug Glazer, two Saskatchewan Teachers Federation mental health counsellors that helped me at the beginning of my heroic journey of healing. As well Mae Stolte and Zeljko Matijevic, two Jungian analysts in Calgary, Alberta gave me their guidance as the journey unfolded. I managed to build a compass with which to make my way along this journey of soul healing with their help.

I must thank my wife. Maureen, who gave me the encouragement to write this story. As I gave her bits and pieces to read as the story unfolded, she was honest in her opinions, something any writer needs if a story is to be worth reading. She waited patiently for this work to be done so that the past could finally be laid to rest. And most importantly, for never giving up on me.

I want to thank my children for never losing faith in me through the difficult years. They never withdrew from my life, even when I made it difficult. They served as motivation to tell the story of the three books that have made up this series of books. I want to give extra thanks to my daughter Noelle for proofing the final version of this book. I kept her red pen busy.

I also want to thank the good people in Elrose and Lanigan for supporting us as friends and neighbours. We all have a community surrounding us, even when we are not aware of that community. I want to thank Kim Temple, the owner of Casa Sorpresas, for providing me with a sacred sanctuary in Puerto Morelos, Mexico where this book was written.

And finally, I want to thank you, the reader, for making it to the end of this journey down a broken road that ended up in a universe of light and hope. That more than anything else, is what motivated me to write the story.

Photos taken on the Journey

My parents, Lucien and Beverly Longpré got married on February 28, 1949. She was sixteen years old and he was seventeen years old. They were married in Ottawa, Ontario, Canada.

My parents and I in late fall, 1949 in Ottawa.

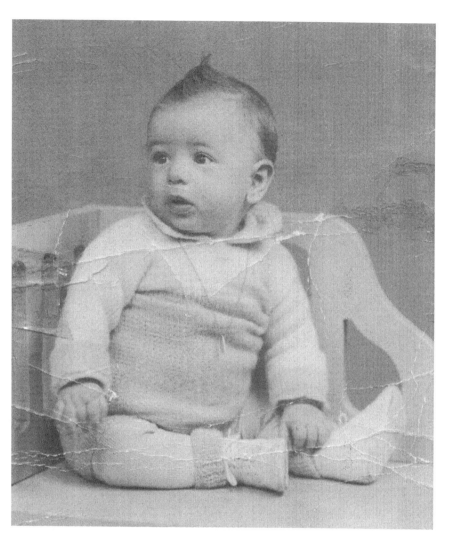

This is me at Christmas time in 1949.

My father on his return from Korea in August, 1951. My brother David was a baby and I was two years old. It was the first time my father had seen David as he was born while my father was in the Far East with the army.

My brothers, David, Larry and Donny with my sister, Bonnie at
Christmas time in 1958. I am holding my youngest brother at that
time, Donny.

My sister Bonnie's First Communion with photo taken at my
mother's parents' house in Ottawa, 1962.

This is my grade ten photo from Ridgemont High School in the early fall of 1965, in Ottawa.

April, 1967 in Sault Ste. Marie where I was an usher for my Uncle Bob's wedding, my mother's second youngest brother.

Christmas at my Uncle Bob's in Vancouver, 1969

Singing Christmas carols on Christmas Eve in Vancouver, 1969.

Our wedding on August 28, 1971 in Edmonton, Alberta.
Maureen's parents were our witnesses in a civil ceremony.

Our wedding photo taken in our basement suite apartment in
Edmonton, Alberta, August 1971.

July, 1973 – We are gardening on the Kohuch farmstead near
Wynyard, Saskatchewan.

The first and last time we had a family photo with all of my siblings.
Photo was taken by Maureen in May, 1974.

Our first child, Noelle in Camsell Portage in northern Saskatchewan where I held my first teaching job. March, 1975.

Our second child, Natasha was born while I was teaching in Sturgeon Landing in Northern Saskatchewan – February, 1977.

Our first two children Noelle and Natasha are in the photo with Maureen's mother and my father. Wynyard, August, 1979.

Our third child, our son, Dustin, was born in Lanigan.
April, 1980

As a family we often went cross-country skiing and finding a place
for a winter picnic – me, Dustin, Noelle and Natasha.
March, 1988.

Family photo Noelle, Dustin, Maureen, me, and Natasha.
Fall, 1990.

Maureen and I in Paris, France at Montmartre, April 1993

Family photo including our son-in-law, Noelle's husband,
celebrating our 25th anniversary and my convocation from my
Master's program in Education from the University of Saskatchewan
Autumn, 1996

The stone sitting in this crude chalice was given to me by Marvin Haave, my STF counsellor just before I went to Calgary for Jungian analysis. The chalice was made by me at a workshop led by Zeljko Matejevic in Calgary while I was in analysis. April 1998.

Maureen and I on a catamaran in Cuba, 2004. The decision to retire had been made. It was time to move on to different things.

Retirement family photo, includes our two sons-in-law and five grandchildren. Elrose, June 2005.

Maureen and I in China singing at the Mayor's Christmas party for foreigners in Changzhou, Jiangsu. December 2006.

At the Taj Mahal in India, January 2008.

On the Great Wall of China near Beijing, April 2008.

Angkor Wat in Cambodia, February, 2011

In the Philippines, meditating in a cave following the death of my
mother in November, 2011.

Maureen and I in Calgary where I am again in Jungian analysis.
February, 2012.

Family photo in August, 2012 including our two sons-in-law, our
daughter-in-law, and our six grandchildren. I have finished Jungian
analysis and am heading out to walk the Camino in France.

Saint Jean Pied de Port, France – the starting point for our Camino
August 26, 2015.

Santiago del Compostela, Spain – the final stop on the Camino de
Santiago, October 2015.

In Paris, France in the Champs de Mars in front of the Eiffel Tower.
October, 2015.

Suggested Readings

Chodron, Pema, The Places That Scare You, 2001
Chodron, Pema, When Things Fall Apart, 2002
Goodson, Aileen, Therapy, Nudity & Joy, 1991
Hollis, James, The Middle Passage, 1993
Hollis, James, Swamplands of the Soul, 1996
Hollis, James, The Eden Project, 1998
Hollis, James, Creating a Life, 2001
Jourard, Sidney, Transparent Self, 1964
Jung, Carl Gustav, Collected Works,
Jung, Carl Gustav, Memories, Dreams, Reflections, 1964
Kornfield, Jack, A Path With Heart, 1993
Moore, Thomas, Care of the Soul, 1988
Moore, Thomas, Soul Mates, 1994
Moore, Thomas, Dark Nights of the Soul, 2004
Nicholson, Ian, "Baring the Soul," Fall 2007
Robinson, Martin, Pilgrim Paths, 1997
Sharp, Daryl, The Survival Papers, 1988
Sharp, Daryl, Dear Gladys, 1989
Sharp, Daryl, Who Am I, Really?, 1995
Trungpa, Chogyam, Smile at Fear, 2009
Trungpa, Chogyam, The Heart of the Buddha, 2010

Made in the USA
Charleston, SC
21 April 2016